# REMEMBERING HANCOCK

REMEMBERING

# HANCOCK

TALES FROM A QUAINT NEW HAMPSHIRE TOWN

CYNTHIA AMIDON

THE History PRESS

Published by The History Press
Charleston, SC 29403
www.historypress.net



*Cover images*: Aerial view of Hancock village. *Courtesy of Deb Porter-Hayes*; Forest Line stagecoach, early 1900s; restored theatre curtain from old town hall, on lower floor of meetinghouse, now stored in the Town Archives. *Courtesy of Deb Porter-Hayes*.

All images are courtesy of the Hancock Historical Society unless otherwise noted.

First published 2010

Manufactured in the United States

ISBN 978.1.59629.410.3

Amidon, Cynthia.
Remembering Hancock : tales from a quaint New Hampshire town / Cynthia Amidon.
p. cm.
ISBN 978-1-59629-410-3
1. Hancock (N.H.)--History--Anecdotes. I. Title.
F44.H4A45 2010
974.2'8--dc22
2010022813

# Contents

# Acknowledgements

Most of these articles appeared first in Hancock's informative and entertaining town newsletter, *Hancock Happenings*, with others printed in *Tintinnabula*, the newsletter of the First Congregational Church, and the *Monadnock Ledger-Transcript* ("Clothespin Factory," "Historical Society Museum in Two-Hundred-Year Old Tavern" and "A Fast Ride in the Dark"). I would like to express my appreciation to *Hancock Happenings* editor Nancy Adams for her many years of tireless effort on behalf of our community, as well as her encouragement and support. To the Hancock Historical Society and to Town Administrator Barbara Caverly—who gave me unlimited access to the treasure-trove of primary source material housed in the town and society archives—thank you for making it possible for me to discover the fascinating people and stories that bring Hancock history to life. Although the majority of the photographs in this work are from the archives of the Hancock Historical Society, several people also generously responded to my plea for additional pictures; their names appear in the relevant captions. Deb Porter-Hayes graciously provided a few of her spectacular photographic images of Hancock to support this project, and Maribeth Sullivan and Bobbie Nylander spent many hours helping with technical details. Bobbie and Ellena Weston share my fascination with Hancock's history and have provided invaluable research assistance as I've written these articles. My husband, Gary Ryer, provided important input on each piece, and his steady support and encouragement helped me put aside other responsibilities to bring this project to completion. My daughter, Jessamyn Dechert, was a great help with grammatical questions and computer issues. Margaret Carlson reviewed this work before it was submitted for publication; thank you, Margaret, for your thoughtful and constructive comments and for your support of my work as a writer. Finally, it is impossible to recognize the many individuals who have labored for decades to preserve and protect the precious archival record of our small town's past, but for me, one Hancock historian stands head and shoulders above the rest. I never would have written a single local history article without the friendship, enthusiasm and encouragement of Gloria Neary, former director and longtime volunteer at the Hancock Historical Society Museum. Thank you, Gloria, for everything.

# INTRODUCTION

It has been almost twenty years since I contributed my first history article to Hancock's monthly community newsletter, *Hancock Happenings*. I had the good fortune to grow up here in Hancock, and from childhood I had an unquenchable curiosity about the history of my hometown. My parents indulged my interest in our community's past, and longtime residents kindly answered my questions and shared their stories, most notably Doris Rogers and Sheilia and Everett Adams. When Nancy Adams gave me the opportunity to contribute a local history column to her new town newsletter, I jumped at the chance to submit stories about Hancock's past for my friends and neighbors to enjoy. The best of my *Hancock Happenings* columns are contained herein, along with a few articles printed first in the newsletter of the First Congregational Church of Hancock, *Tintinnabula*, and in the *Monadnock Ledger-Transcript*.

One of the great pleasures in writing these monthly columns has been the opportunity to range freely through the rich archival storehouse of Hancock's past, selecting and delving into the incidents, individuals and buildings that pique my interest. Having gathered sufficient information on a subject to satisfy my curiosity, I work hard to write about it in a way that will attract and engage the attention of my mostly local audience. I truly believe that shared stories such as these help bring us together as a community. They remind us that, as proud as we all are of Hancock's picturesque, historic village and the beauty of our natural landscape, it isn't what our community looks like that matters—it is who we are. The town we all enjoy living in and visiting today is the product of generations before us who worked hard, made difficult choices and sometimes had to place the needs of their community ahead of their own desires. This is the gift of local history: the opportunity to remember where we've been and how we got here and to use that knowledge to help us make good decisions about what we want our town to be like in the future. As you'll see in the following pages, this much has always been true: life in Hancock hasn't been easy, but we've still managed to have a good time. We've worried about major decisions, yet we've also paid attention to the small details that have yielded a surprisingly rich and vibrant community culture. This town has endured because of people who have cared deeply about its welfare and feel personally invested in its future.

I appreciate the opportunity to bring these stories about Hancock's past to a wider audience, with the help of The History Press. I sincerely hope that this book inspires others with a passion for local history to explore, record and share the unique stories of their own communities. Future generations will be glad you did.

# Part I

# Friends and Neighbors

## The Church v. Lieutenant Joseph Symonds

When Benjamin Abbot took issue with the behavior of prominent Hancock citizen Joseph Symonds in 1802, he didn't take his complaint to the local court. Rather, he brought it to the First Congregational Church, of which Joseph Symonds was one of the founding members. Abbot initially accused Symonds of eight separate incidents of slander and misrepresentation; after due consideration, the church members ultimately decided to act on only one. An account of the ensuing "case" is one of several documented in the *Records of the Church of Christ in Hancock; Volume 1; Anno Domini 1792.*

According to the 1829 *Ratio Disciplinæ, or the Constitution of the Congregational Churches*, it was appropriate for churches to take on cases of "reproof and censure" in the local community when one of their members was involved. "Offending brethren" might be "reclaimed," others who might be tempted to engage in similar behavior deterred and, if necessary, action undertaken "for purging out the leaven, which may infect the whole lump." Such action would, of course, "vindicate the honor of Christ," as well as prevent the wrath of God from descending on congregations allowing themselves to be "profaned by notorious and obstinate offenders."

A Paul Revere bell installed in newly rebuilt meetinghouse in 1820. *Photo by Eleanor Briggs. Courtesy of Town of Hancock.*

For the next two years, church brethren and Reverend Reed Paige grappled with the remaining "charge" against Symonds. A proud veteran of the Revolutionary War, Symonds apparently enjoyed reminiscing about his days serving as a lieutenant in the young nation's army. But according to Abbot, Symonds was, in fact, an army deserter who had been heard to falsely claim that he had hired a substitute to take his place so that he could return home. For months, the elders of the church listened to witnesses, considered the evidence and met with the accused. Finally, they decided that if Symonds would confess that he did in fact "leave the army without leaving a good man in his stead," no further action would be taken against him. Symonds steadfastly refused to do so, and in November 1803 a disheartened Reverend Paige was forced to send a letter of excommunication to his longtime friend.

Excommunication was the Congregational Church's harshest punishment, but it was careful to delineate the limits of such an action in its *Constitution*. Excommunication was considered a "spiritual punishment"; it didn't deprive former members of their civil rights or even of their presence at church. Their new status was likened to that of "heathens," who were "lawfully permitted to come to hear the word."

We don't know if, in fact, Joseph Symonds ever attended the Hancock Church again, although we do know that his wife and children continued to be active members throughout their lives.

Town meeting and tax records make it plain that the community of Hancock also took Symonds's censure by the Church seriously. For the rest of his life, Symonds was officially referred to as *Esquire* Joseph Symonds, instead of *Lieutenant* Joseph Symonds, as he had been previously. But when the Paul Revere bell was rung for the first time in the steeple of the newly rebuilt meetinghouse, jointly owned by the Congregational Society and the Town of Hancock, it was to toll the sad news of the death of one of their own. Joseph Symonds died on October 15, 1820, at the age of seventy-four. Writing sixty years later in *The History of Hancock, New Hampshire, 1764–1889*, historian William Willis Hayward remembered Symonds as "much respected in town, a man of sterling qualities of character."

## Hard Times for a Woman Alone

The intrepid settlers who left established farms in settled communities for the rugged uplands of eighteenth-century Hancock led lives of unrelenting toil and economic uncertainty. This was particularly true of the unfortunate women who, through death or abandonment, found themselves alone.

Margaret Walker Margery, known as Peggy, was one early Hancock woman whose story is particularly compelling. Peggy and her husband, Jonathan, a veteran of the Revolutionary War, came to Hancock prior to 1788, when Jonathan appears in the town records as one of the petitioners for a new road near King's Highway. It is believed that the Margerys lived between Lake Nubanusit and Shadrach Pond; a cellar hole is still visible there.

By 1801, however, Jonathan Margery had left his family and, according to Hancock historian William Willis Hayward, "was not heard from, but the horse he went away with came back three years later alone."

Peggy was fifty-one years old when her husband left; left to her own resources, she became a professional weaver. Weaving was one of the few occupations then available to single women; they would produce cloth from the yarn spun in neighboring households, usually in exchange for goods or other services since cash was scarce. Although Peggy's son, Andrew, married in 1806 and settled either on the homestead or nearby, by 1812 he had died, and his young widow had remarried and moved away. Peggy's daughter, Ellenor, had also married but had left Hancock with her husband for New York State.

Eventually, Peggy could no longer work to support herself, and with no surviving family nearby she became a ward of the town. As was common practice, the town of Hancock assumed ownership of her property, and her support was auctioned off annually at town meetings. At some point, Peggy Margery moved to the Hancock Poor Farm on Nahor Hill; she died there of "Palsey" in 1836 at age eighty-six.

## Journal of an All-Too-Brief Life: Olive Hills (1792–1823)

If her journal hadn't been preserved, all we'd know about Olive Hills is that she was born in Hancock in 1792 and lived on the farm her father cleared on Nahor Hill (the discontinued road that begins where North Road intersects with High Street) until her death in 1823 at thirty-one years of age. But thanks to her homemade diary—twenty-nine hand-sewn pages covered with ancient wallpaper—we can find out quite a bit more about this young woman and her life in Hancock.

The journal begins on November 30, 1818, when Olive was twenty-six years old and just beginning a new course of study with a private teacher in Hancock. These private schools were often the only opportunity for those desiring education beyond the elementary level; Olive attended at least three of them for several weeks each during the interval covered by her diary. She was an eager student who preferred studying arithmetic, polite literature, grammar, geography and "perspicuity" to punctuation, which she considered dull. She worried over her composition on "The Grand Division of Asia" and lamented the close of every session of school and the passing of the many happy hours spent there. Olive refers to her fellow classmates as "companions" and her teachers as "Miss N.," "Miss Lawrence" and "Mr. C."

Olive was also an active participant in her religious education, carefully noting the text of each week's sermon and responding to it in her diary. She

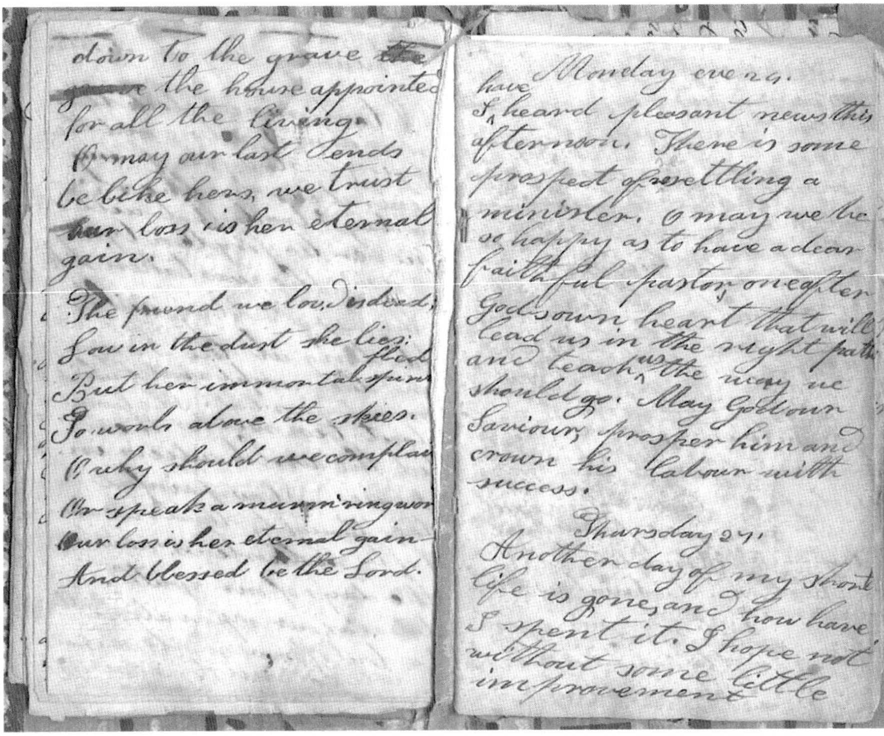
down to the grave the
the house appointed
for all the living.
O may our last ends
be like hers, we trust
her loss is her eternal
gain.
The friend we lov'd is dead;
Low in the dust she lies:
But her immortal spirit fled
To worlds above the skies.
O why should we complain
Or speak a murmuring word
Our loss is her eternal gain
And blessed be the Lord.

Monday even'g.
I have heard pleasant news this
afternoon. There is some
prospect of settling a
minister. O may we be
so happy as to have a dear
faithful pastor, one after
God's own heart that will
lead us in the right path
and teach us the way we
should go. May God our
Saviour prosper him and
crown his labour with
success.
Thursday 27.
Another day of my short
life is gone, and how have
I spent it. I hope not
without some little
improvement

Olive Hills's journal.

was writing during an interval following the death of Reverend Reed Paige when the Congregational Church in Hancock lacked a settled minister, so Olive often traveled to nearby Antrim to hear Reverend Whiton preach. She also attended prayer meetings and went to hear missionaries speak on their travels. It is with a sad hand that she writes on Thursday, October 28, 1819:

> *This day about 12 o clock I heard the unexpected news that our Meetinghouse was in flames, the news spread over town very fast, and in a short amount of time the people collected there, but alas; it was all in vain; the house was laid in ruins before our eyes. The wind was very high the flames spread rapidly on till it was in ashes…now our earthly sanctuary is no more.*

Just one year later, Olive attended the dedication of the new meetinghouse on October 25, 1820.

Despite the evident enjoyment Olive took in her studies and occasional comments on particularly fine weather and happy hours spent with family and friends, the diary also records an ongoing preoccupation with her own mortality. This isn't particularly surprising given the frequency of the funerals of neighbors and friends that dot its pages, along with the illnesses and tragic losses of family members. Olive helped nurse a nephew through the devastating dysentery epidemic of 1819, and a brother-in-law almost perished from "typhus fever" in 1820. Her twenty-year-old sister Miriam died in 1821; a particularly heartbreaking, tear-stained page records the death of Olive's mother, Hannah, of consumption (tuberculosis) on August 3, 1822. This is the final page of Olive's diary; she died the following January, two days before her sister, Hannah, and a year before her sister, Phebe, quite possibly of tuberculosis, the same illness that took so many others from her family. As she wrote at the death of her sister Miriam:

*Diseases are thy servants Lord;*
*They come at thy command;*
*I'll not attempt a murmuring word*
*Against thy chastening hand.*

## JAMES HOSLEY WHITCOMB: NINETEENTH-CENTURY SILHOUETTIST

When James Hosley Whitcomb lost his hearing during a bout of scarlet fever in early childhood, it must have been a blow to his family, already prominent local residents in 1809. They knew that rural communities like Hancock didn't offer many options for those whose futures were compromised due to illness or disability. But through a fortunate sequence of events, Whitcomb's deafness led to his greatest opportunity and ensured his legacy as a nineteenth-century "profile cutter," or silhouettist.

According to research done in the 1970s by Donna-Belle Garvin of the New Hampshire Historical Society and published in volume 32 of *Historical New Hampshire*, Whitcomb was one of nine deaf New Hampshire children fortunate enough to receive a legislative scholarship in 1822 to attend the new American Asylum in Hartford, Connecticut. Founded in 1817 for the education of deaf-

Whitcomb silhouettes in the collection of the Hancock Historical Society. In the top center is Reverend John P. Hills; in the upper right is Lucy Boyd Kimball; and in the lower right is Asa Washburn. The others are unidentified.

mutes, this school was the first of its kind, and it combined a classical education with career preparation. Although Whitcomb trained as a shoemaker, the unusual number of known artists who graduated from this program indicates that he may have benefited from some fine arts education there as well.

By the early 1830s, Whitcomb had already achieved some success as an itinerant silhouette cutter, producing images of men and women living in his native Hancock and beyond. Silhouettes were a popular means of preserving and sharing individual likenesses when painted portraits were prohibitively expensive and photographic techniques were crude and not widely available. Known examples of Whitcomb's work are mostly of the "hollow-cut" type: the outline of the sitter's head and bust, or "profile," is cut out of white paper that is then mounted against a piece of black fabric. Additional details, identifying inscriptions and/or the artist's signature are added to the paper surface in ink. Whitcomb eventually settled in New York State, where he married Sarah Enos, also a deaf-mute, and had three children. He died there in 1849 at the age of forty-three.

The New Hampshire Historical Society has several examples of Whitcomb's work, one of which is a signed self-portrait done in 1831. The Hancock Historical Society has a few Whitcomb silhouettes featuring local residents; others can be found in private collections.

## A FATHER'S WARNING TO THE UNWARY

In the early 1800s, the residents of Hancock relied on their weekly newspapers both for entertainment and to keep them informed about local, regional and national issues. The most popular newspapers among Hancock readers were the *Farmer's Cabinet*, published in Amherst, and the *New Hampshire Patriot*, published in Concord. Knowing that the information in these papers would reach a large audience, one angry Hancock father took advantage of the opportunity to place an unusual advertisement in the February 2, 1824 issue of the *New Hampshire Patriot*:

> *BEWARE OF WOLVES IN SHEEP'S CLOTHING*
>
> *The subscriber deems it to be a duty to the Public, and Females in particular, to beware a man by the name of IRA ALLEN. Said Allen came to this town something like two years ago, and hired himself to work out as a journeyman at the Axe and Blacksmithing business. Being a good workman, and appearing to be industrious and steady, he acquired the confidence of his acquaintance. A few months after he came to Hancock he became acquainted with a worthy young woman of respectable connections, and feigned himself as a widower. He was married to her about a year since. Since which time he has lived with said wife in this place until about three weeks ago when he absconded. It is ascertained that a few years since he married a woman at St. Johnsbury in Vermont, by whom he had two children. He afterwards left her and went to Marlborough in the state of Vermont where he enticed a young girl to marry him under false pretences of having been divorced from his former wife who was then alive. He lived with his second wife about three years more than one of which was while his first wife lived. She is since dead. His second wife resides in Marlborough, Vermont, in very indigent circumstances, encumbered with three small children, the offspring of her connection with said Allen. He left his said wife and children when*

George Franklin Allen. *Courtesy of Suzanne Gagnon.*

*he came to this town, and it was not until before three or four weeks since that his family first heard of his being in this place. Immediately after Allen found out his true character was known here he absconded and it is not known where he now is. Said Allen is about 37 or 38 years of age, dark complexion, dark hair, short in stature and round shouldered. Printers in this and other states are requested to give the above one or more insertions as it is believed that the public good requires that such infamy should be exposed.*

*James Hills*

*Hancock, NH Dec. 24, 1823.*

As documented in the town records, James Hills's daughter, Abigail, married Ira Allen on December 26, 1822; she was thirty years old. She bore a son, George Franklin Allen, on February 28, 1824; by the date of his baptism, she was listed as "divorced." On October 14, 1848, she arrived at the Hancock Poor Farm "with nothing except her wareing apparel"; she died there a little over a year later at age fifty-seven and is buried at the Pine Ridge Cemetery.

According to descendant Suzanne Gagnon, who has done substantial genealogical research on the Allen family, it is evident from surviving correspondence in her collection that the Hills family continued to search unsuccessfully for Ira Allen for some years. George Franklin Allen grew up in Hancock and married Sarah Ann Miller, a young woman whose own father, ironically, had also long since abandoned his family. George died in Nashua in 1910.

## Bound for Gold in California

The discovery of gold in California in 1848 did not go unnoticed in the small community of Hancock. Several local men soon joined those undertaking the long and perilous journey to California via ship around Cape Horn, in the hope of making their fortunes. Many never again returned to Hancock; one was so successful that his generous legacy to his native town endures today.

John Copeland Weston grew up in Hancock but was apparently infected with wanderlust at an early age. In 1851, he left Boston on the ship *John Wade* as a "sailor before the mast," sailing around the world before returning to New England a year later. He relocated to California in 1853 and then later to Iowa, where he lived out the rest of his life, still maintaining an active interest in his hometown. In 1904, he shared recollections of his youth with the Hancock Historical Society.

According to Weston, it was a sailor named John Bixby, residing in the building that now houses the society's museum, who "turned the minds" of Hancock's young men toward California. Bixby had recently returned from a voyage there and "was an object of much interest…listened to by eager groups in stores, and elsewhere." Weston remembered visiting the sailor in

John Copeland Weston, taken in California in the 1850s. *Courtesy of Weston family.*

his rented room on the second floor, where Bixby "(having learned the art on shipboard)…tattooed a date, and emblem, with needles and India ink, on the tender skin of my arm," still visible more than fifty years later.

Abel B. Winship was the first Hancock resident to strike out for California; he returned bearing a specimen of "native gold." Several others soon followed, including Weston's brother, James, who died on the journey under mysterious circumstances and was buried at sea. Timothy Paige, son of Hancock's first minister, abruptly left a promising career in the U.S. Army to head west in 1848; he landed a lucrative position in the San Francisco Post Office. Weston bumped into him there on his voyage around the world in 1852.

Hancock brothers Adolphus C. and Charles A. Whitcomb moved to California after graduating together from Harvard Law School in 1849. Although Charles died just two years later from burns received during the Great San Francisco Fire, Adolphus was able to acquire a "handsome fortune" in California. He left a significant bequest to his hometown of Hancock, his legacy most visible today in the attractive façade of the library, erected in 1882. Charles is remembered by a picture painted for him by his mother prior to her own untimely death from consumption, hanging today in the society's museum.

Altogether, Weston lists the names of forty-seven Hancock residents who he knew had left town for California, beginning with the gold rush of 1848. "I myself have known of many, and am convinced that more have gone, than from any other place whatever, in proportion to the population."

## Orland Eaton Founded Hancock Historical Society

Born in 1836, Orland Eaton was the grandson of one of Hancock's first settlers, Lemuel Eaton, who came here in 1791. He lived on the family homestead on Eaton Road, now the home of Penny English, which under his stewardship became one of the finest fruit farms in Hancock. At the 1886 town fair, Eaton exhibited twenty-five varieties of apples, ten varieties of pears and nineteen varieties of grapes.

Eaton devoted a great deal of time and energy to the community of Hancock throughout his lifetime, serving on many important town and church committees. One of his most enduring contributions was donating the land and pipe access necessary for the town water system; he removed the first shovelful of earth in the groundbreaking ceremonies in 1907.

Orland and Nellie (Davis) Eaton.

Passionate about preserving the history of his town, Eaton was instrumental in coordinating the centennial celebration in 1879 and served as chairman of the town history committee that published *History of Hancock, New Hampshire, 1764–1889*. He was also the leader of a small group that collected the early documents and artifacts that became the basis of the collection of the Hancock Historical Society, incorporated May 9, 1903. The society was founded with twenty-eight charter members; Eaton served as the first president and continued in that position until his death in 1910.

# FAMOUS AMERICAN ARTIST PAINTED IN HANCOCK

In late summer of 1931, local residents were treated to a two-week art exhibit at Hancock High School, featuring twenty-nine portraits and landscapes painted by their "distinguished fellow townswoman," Lilla Cabot Perry. According to the September 3 issue of the *Peterborough Transcript*, the exhibit "attracted many visitors," who particularly enjoyed the portraits of familiar local residents and "scenes of Norway Hill and Mount Skatutakee… beautiful in their autumn colorings."

By 1931, Lilla Cabot Perry was nearing the end of a painting career that had begun when she was a young mother of three living in Boston. Perry's mother was a Lowell and her father a Cabot; she was raised in a patrician Boston family whose circle regularly included such literary luminaries as Louisa May Alcott and Ralph Waldo Emerson. It was one of her close friends, the author Henry James, who first introduced her to the man she would marry in 1874, a Harvard-educated literary scholar and linguist, Thomas Sergeant Perry. Although the union of Cabot and Perry (a direct descendant of Benjamin Franklin and grandson of Commodore Oliver Hazard Perry) "unquestionably united two families of impeccable lineage and proved to be extremely close, it was not one that united two fortunes," according to Meredith Martindale, whose biography *Lilla Cabot Perry: An American Impressionist* was published to accompany a 1990 exhibit of Perry's work at the Washington, D.C. National Museum of Women in the Arts.

Despite her husband's sporadic employment as a teacher and contributor to literary journals, it was Perry's small inheritance supplemented by her portrait painting that supported the couple and their three children for much of their lives. Remembered as one of Boston's most distinguished artists, Perry honed her skills through study with prominent painters in America and abroad. She received a great deal of critical acclaim during her lifetime for her portraiture but is perhaps most remembered for the impressionist works she produced during ten years spent summering in Giverny, France, beginning in 1889.

It was less expensive to maintain her family's lifestyle in France than in Boston, and Paris was a popular destination for writers and artists in the late nineteenth century. It was Perry's close friendships with impressionist painters Claude Monet and Camille Pissarro that led her to experiment

Oil Paintings
*by*
Lilla Cabot Perry

Hancock High School
August 20th to 29th
2 to 5 p. m.

Art exhibit program.

with this new style of painting—she was very influential in bringing it to the attention of American audiences. Although Monet didn't take pupils, he frequently advised Perry on her work, telling her "to paint what you really see, not what you think you ought to see." One of Perry's paintings still hangs in Monet's bedroom in Giverny, and she was one of the best-represented artists at the World's Columbian Exposition in Chicago in 1893, the most important cultural event of the era and considered a "triumph" for impressionism in America.

Following a three-year stay in Japan, where Perry's husband taught at a university in Tokyo, the couple purchased a home in Hancock, already a popular summer destination for upper-class Bostonians. They enjoyed the proximity to other "cultural elites" in nearby Dublin and Peterborough and the outstanding natural scenery that included Mount Monadnock. Her husband is quoted in a November 1990 article in *Victoria* magazine as saying that Hancock was "a spot nearer Heaven by about 1,100 feet than Boston or Beverly." The Perrys bought the 250-acre Tuttle Farm, soon renamed Flagstones by family friend and frequent visitor Henry James, and from 1910 on they spent part of every year there surrounded by family and friends. Frequent visitors included William Dean Howells, the poet Edwin Arlington Robinson and artist Frederick Bosley, among others.

Two of Perry's daughters also maintained homes nearby; Margaret Perry lived in Hancock year-round and maintained a purebred dairy herd on the family acreage. Alice de Vermandois Grew and her husband, prominent American diplomat Joseph Clark Grew, owned two properties adjacent to Flagstones farm that were popular destinations for their own extended family. All three properties remain in the family today, along with Perry's small, shingled studio, retained much as she left it and located adjacent to the farmhouse in a nearby meadow.

Perry continued to paint throughout her life; the paintings she did of Hancock in her later years are considered among her finest works. Poetry was another lifelong passion; she published four volumes of her poems, including *Impression: A Book of Verse* in 1898 and *The Jar of Dreams* in 1923. Examples of her paintings can be found in major museums in both the United States and Europe and in many private collections; one of her pieces depicting a local youth fishing from a rustic footbridge adorned the White House during the Clinton years. A portrait of prominent local resident Ella Goodhue, along with a charming painting of an unknown young woman, can be seen locally in the Hancock Town Library, and the Hancock Historical Society owns a painting from Perry's Tokyo years, *Daughter of Baron O.*

According to family recollections published in Martindale's biography, Perry was working on a landscape of Crotched Mountain when she passed away on February 28, 1933, at age eighty-six. She died here in her beloved Hancock—the town, she once wrote, that "embodied 'the soul' of the New England landscape, as seen through Emerson's eyes."

## EMMA COOLIDGE WESTON FOUNDED NEW HAMPSHIRE ASSOCIATION FOR THE BLIND

The New Hampshire Association for the Blind, founded nearly one hundred years ago in 1912, "is dedicated to enhancing the quality of life and maximizing

Emma A. (Weston) Coolidge and F.E. Duncan, 1890.

independence for Granite State residents who experience blindness and visual impairment." According to its mission, the nonprofit organization provides rehabilitative services, creates a "climate of acceptance" for the blind and visually impaired so that they might live independent lives and, finally, fosters philanthropic support of services to meet the needs of these New Hampshire residents.

This organization, now based in Concord, originated in Hancock in 1912 as the creation of a small group of blind individuals headed by Mrs. Emma Coolidge Weston. Weston and her friends were concerned at the lack of state services provided for blind and visually impaired New Hampshire residents and were determined to remedy the situation.

According to a memoir penned by her daughter, longtime *Peterborough Transcript* and *Manchester Union Leader* correspondent Nancy West, Emma Adelia Coolidge was born in Massachusetts in 1857. During her first year of life, Emma lost all but 10 percent of her sight due to a bout of whooping cough. As the daughter of a Methodist minister, Emma moved many times during her childhood and so was exposed to a great variety of places and people. Her daughter writes that Emma's family took advantage of every opportunity to encourage her to develop and utilize her active mind. Emma loved to write; some of her work was published at an early age in the then popular *Youth's Companion*.

The Coolidge family moved to Hancock when Emma was fourteen years old; at age eighteen, she entered the Perkins Institution for the Blind in Boston, with her tuition paid for by the State of New Hampshire. That was the only state assistance available to blind and visually impaired New Hampshire residents at that time. After graduation from the Massachusetts State Normal School in Fitchburg, Massachusetts, with highest honors (and as the first blind student to complete a course in an advanced school), Emma studied for a year at Wellesley College, also in Massachusetts. She then took a job as teacher at the Perkins School for several years. West notes that one of her mother's better-known pupils was Anne Sullivan, who later went on to teach Helen Keller. Emma left her teaching career in 1891 to marry Hancock resident James T. Weston.

To assist in the support of her family, Emma took in blind children from the Perkins School as summer boarders. She also began to knit professionally, a skill she had learned at the Perkins Institute. When Weston received orders for her work from the Massachusetts Commission for the Blind, she realized the potential for a similar organization in New Hampshire. In 1912, she gathered together a group of blind friends, including a legislative representative from Manchester, Henry J. VanVliet, to discuss the possibility of forming a state association for the blind in New Hampshire. It was determined that such an organization should be founded, with a local chapter in each town. Early officers of the Hancock branch included Reverend Frank Pearson and W.M. Davis, in addition to Emma herself. An Organization Fair was held in the Hancock Town Hall, with a sale of donated articles, as well as items made by blind individuals in both New Hampshire and Massachusetts.

The following winter, the New Hampshire legislature approved a $5,000 annual appropriation to fund a commission for the blind under the board of public welfare. The Hancock branch continued for a time, with the support of summer residents such as Mrs. Henry Tudor, among others. Eventually, the local groups disbanded, but the New Hampshire Association for the Blind was officially incorporated in 1933, centrally located in Concord, where it continues to thrive today. Emma Weston died in 1939, but her belief in the potential for the blind and visually impaired to lead normal, productive lives endures in this successful statewide organization.

## *That Darned Minister's Son*: Haydn Pearson

In the spring of 1908, a Congregational minister's young wife and four children arrived in Hancock to join him on his newly purchased farm. Having spent a long and dusty day traveling via train from Maine, the tired Pearson family finally embarked on the last leg of their journey via horse and buggy from the Hancock Depot to Glenrose Farm on Middle Hancock Road. Eight-year-old Haydn later wrote about that important day:

> *We drove down the road to the village, saw the imposing, tall, beautiful white church and the red brick vestry, the common and the bandstand, turned down Sand Hill, and jogged out along the Valley road…it was deepening dusk as we turned into the yard. I remember the golden bands of lamp light shining into the yard from the kitchen windows. We trooped into the low-ceilinged kitchen. The black nickel-plated Home Comfort range had a cheerful crackling fire. There was a big pot of stew simmering on the second cover and a pan of rolls heating in the oven, The oilcloth-covered table was heaped with pies, cakes, ham, and bacon…"The neighbors came in this afternoon," Father said, "Wouldn't stay, just welcomed us." That was the family's introduction to Hancock.*

A war-weary America in the 1940s and 1950s relished the nostalgic writings of Haydn Pearson, who grew up to author articles for such periodicals as the *Newark Sunday News*, the *Rural New Yorker*, the *Milking Shorthorn Journal*, the *Worcester Sunday Telegram* and the *Peterborough Transcript*, along with writing several books. In his work, Pearson drew heavily on his memories of childhood years spent happily in Hancock helping on the family farm and participating in community activities such as Old Home Day and the Greenfield Fair.

While light and frequently humorous, his books and articles also contain many important clues about what life was like in Hancock early in the past

Pearson farm on Middle Hancock Road.

century. Present-day readers will recognize many familiar local landmarks mentioned by Pearson, including Norway Pond, Mount Skatutakee and the Grange Hall (now post office). References are also made to long-gone town fixtures, such as the blacksmith shop at the foot of Norway Hill and the one-room district schoolhouses. It doesn't take too much imagination to picture young Haydn and his friends trailing after the old lamplighter as he made his way down Main Street each evening, hand-lighting each kerosene streetlight, or the bandstand softly lit by lanterns as the Hancock Cornet Band entertained townspeople on a summer night.

Although currently out of print, Pearson's books *That Darned Minister's Son* and *Countryman's Year* and his cookbooks *The Countryman's Cookbook* and *Country Flavor* all contain references to Hancock and can be found at local libraries for cozy and entertaining winter reading. Those of us who might be tempted to treat the information they contain as verifiable historical fact, however, would do well to heed Pearson's own warning in the conclusion to his introduction to *That Darned Minister's Son*, which he dedicated to the people of Hancock:

*To you who were and who still are the strength of New Hampshire's granite-studded hills, I offer my gratitude. Some of these stories you know; some will clear up mysteries. Most of what I am going to write is the truth. Some of it will be seasoned with a whiffle of imagination and a smidgen of exaggeration. A small portion is entirely fictional.*

## An Exiled Prince and his Birds

Prince Irakly Toumanoff, claiming a royal lineage that went back nine centuries into Persian history, served as a colonel in the Imperial Russian Guard during World War I. Wounded three times on the front lines, surely the most grievous blow he received was when the czar was overthrown and the new Bolshevik government declared the prince an enemy of state. After a tumultuous interval in Turkey, where the Toumanoff family struggled to evade arrest and certain death at the hands of the communists, they fled to America in 1923. They lived as refugees for a few years in New York before moving to Boston in 1927. Shortly thereafter, they discovered Hancock. Toumanoff, his wife and his young sons found peace and some measure of financial security on a small farm on Weston Road, now the home of Ken and Heidi Chester.

Toumanoff's fascinating story is recounted by his son in *An Interview with Vladimir I. Toumanoff*, published by the Association for Diplomatic Studies and Training Foreign Affairs Oral History Project, Foreign Affairs Series, in 2000. While living in New York, Prince Toumanoff had made his living with his violin, playing in restaurants and hotels, and had worked in a ginger ale bottling factory. His wife, well educated and fluent in multiple languages, taught school and worked in social services. A talented vocalist, she performed with her husband at concerts during the winter at his home in Boston, as well as in Hancock during the summer months.

Toumanoff also found another, novel way to contribute to his family's support during their summers in Hancock. He raised birds for the table—first turkeys and geese and then "game birds" such as partridges, mallard ducks and pheasants. Although he claimed no prior experience raising birds, he received such acclaim for his innovative methods that he was selected to address other poultrymen at a New Hampshire

Birds on the Toumanoff farm.

Cooperative Extension Program in 1934. According to an article written about the presentation in the December 14, 1934 issue of the *Boston Post,* Toumanoff liked raising poultry because he could farm in the summer and then return to the city for the winter. At that time, he was marketing as many as three hundred turkeys, three hundred ducks and one hundred geese annually, mostly by mail order.

In the archives at the Hancock Historical Society is an undated brochure advertising *Hootor Game Farm* ("hootor" is the Russian term for a one-man farm on the outskirts of a village). Inside are three beautiful feathers, one for each of the advertised birds: "Extra large and meaty Pheasants" (five dollars per pair), "Rock (Chukar) Partridges, a delicious delicacy" (four dollars per pair) and "Wild Mallard Ducks, raised in captivity, very tender" (three dollars per pair). All the birds were advertised as "spring hatched, raised especially for table use, dry picked, perfectly dressed, and ready to cook, with free delivery." Toumanoff raised all of his birds from egg to table on his Weston Road farm.

Toumanoff's affection for the late czar and his family are apparent in a fascinating talk he gave to the Hancock Historical Society in 1930 on the mysterious Rasputin, a man he claimed to have come very close to personally assassinating while a military officer in Russia. He said he was "very glad" to have the opportunity to speak about the imperial family, "whom I had the happiness to know rather intimately and the honor to serve." He also appreciated the chance to enlighten his friends in Hancock about the realities of the situation in Russia, a topic about which he felt Americans knew all too little.

The Toumanoff family still maintains a close connection with the town; they own property and a summer home near the site of their former farm on Weston Road. In a 1986 interview, Hancock native and longtime resident Karl Upton remembered Irakly Toumanoff as a "good citizen, and he could play the sweetest violin that I ever heard."

## Kay's Christmas Tree and Worm Farm

Fifty years ago, in Hancock as in much of northern New England, there were quite a few fallow farm fields growing up into brush. People who wanted to keep some of their land open without grazing livestock began looking around for other options. One "new" alternative that rapidly became popular was growing conifer trees that could be marketed directly at the farm as "cut your own" Christmas trees. Conifers grew well on acid soil, didn't mind the harsh climate and required less maintenance than regular crops or livestock. Customers liked them because they were pruned into a prettier tree than could typically be found in the nearby woods. By the 1960s, cut-your-own Christmas tree "farms" were providing a nice income for farmers and retirees throughout New England. The first person in this area to raise Christmas trees was Hancock's own Kay Moore.

Moore had spent summers in Hancock as a child, moving here permanently in 1913 when her parents bought a farm at the end of Longview Road. She eventually inherited the property, sharing it with her cousins Dell and Jim Eva, with whom she'd spend holidays and summer vacations. When Moore retired to Hancock in 1961 after thirty-five years of teaching in Winsted, Connecticut, she decided to reclaim part of the farm and grow Christmas trees. Bill Eva, whose family lives on the farm now, estimates that Moore planted one and a half to two acres of balsam, Colorado blue spruce and red spruce, which she maintained pretty much

Kay Moore in 2003. *Courtesy of Barbara Caverly.*

on her own, although Bill's dad, Jim, may have helped out occasionally. Every December for several years Moore would don her winter wear and greet customers with a smile and a saw as they all trooped out to choose the perfect tree for their family celebration.

Moore also had another "farm" project: she built and managed a "worm emporium." In 1962, she ordered five thousand "Red Gold Hybrid" worms from Texas. She kept her worms in large, concrete block–lined pits that were built so sturdily that they serve as the foundation for Eva's sugarhouse today. There Moore tended her worms, feeding them every two weeks with cornmeal, coffee grounds and chick feed. She sold them for a penny apiece in quantities of fifty to one hundred for use in compost piles and by fishermen. Her largest single order was for four thousand worms; it took her two days to count them all out. In 1962 and 1963, she sold twelve to fifteen thousand of her red worms each season. Unfortunately, Moore's worm enterprise failed after the recommended treatment to eradicate moles (an earthworm farmer's greatest enemy) apparently killed all the worms as well.

When asked about her unusual farming enterprise in a 1963 article in the *Peterborough Transcript*, Moore replied that "[i]t's just something for a retired school teacher to do for fun." Moore died in April 2007 at the age of 102.

## Hancock Ambassador Warned of Pearl Harbor Attack

On January 27, 1941, U.S. Ambassador to Tokyo Joseph C. Grew sent a dispatch to President Franklin D. Roosevelt at the White House. Grew had received a tip that the Japanese were planning a massive surprise attack on American forces stationed at Pearl Harbor. Whether the warning was never received or was simply ignored remains a topic of intense debate among historians, according to FDR biographer Doris Kearns Goodwin. Grew had been the United States Ambassador to Japan for ten years prior to the attack on Pearl Harbor in December 1941, the culminating post in a forty-one-year foreign service career that had also taken his family to Cairo, Mexico, Russia, Berlin, Vienna, Denmark, Switzerland and Istanbul. From 1923 until his death in 1965, Ambassador Grew's legal residence was here in Hancock.

Grew was raised in Boston, where he haunted the nearby docks to indulge his "early love of ships and the youthful visions of foreign seas and ports," according to his memoir, *Turbulent Era: A Diplomatic Record of Forty Years 1904–1945*. Educated at Groton and Harvard, Grew risked parental ire when he rejected the family tradition of banking or business, choosing instead to pursue a career in the diplomatic service. A devoted fan of the writings of Rudyard Kipling, it was his own book about hunting tigers on a post-graduation, round-the-world trip that first brought Grew to the attention of President Teddy Roosevelt. Roosevelt appointed him to his first foreign service post in Cairo in 1904.

In 1905, Grew married Alice de Vermandois Perry, daughter of Boston Brahmin and literary scholar Thomas Sergeant Perry and famed American impressionist painter Lilla Cabot Perry. According to Grew biographer

The residence of Ambassador Joseph C. Grew.

Waldo H. Heinrichs Jr., Alice Perry "was all an aspiring diplomat could wish for in a wife." She was beautiful, cultured and well traveled, having lived for three years in Japan while her father taught at a university there. In 1904, the Perrys had purchased Tuttle Farm, located at 34 Kings Highway, where they spent many happy summers with their children and grandchildren. In 1923, the Grews purchased two adjacent properties to serve as "home base" for their family when they were in America.

Grew, his wife and his four daughters lived "comfortably and fashionably" at his various posts around the world, according to Heinrichs. Entertaining was an essential component of diplomacy; Grew also enjoyed athletic pursuits such as tennis, skiing and hunting. By all accounts a close family that enjoyed spending time together, the Grews were devastated by the sudden loss of their eldest daughter, Edith, who succumbed to scarlet fever while on a school trip to Vienna in 1924. Alice Grew had her own close call with mortality, becoming deathly ill while the family was posted to Mexico. She was rushed back to Boston where, fortunately, she recovered, although she never fully regained her health.

According to her granddaughter, Lilla Lyon, this episode, possibly triggered by altitude sickness, was partly why the Grews preferred summers in Manchester-by-the-Sea instead of in Hancock. Grew had also spent boyhood summers in the coastal enclave, and they had many friends and family members nearby. Yet the Grews retained the house at 19 Grew Drive and a guest cottage known as "Birch Ridge," now the home of Jim and Polly Curran at 8 Grew Drive, for the rest of their lives. A 1940 issue of the *Manchester Union* noted that all three of their surviving daughters had followed their parents' lead and married into "Uncle Sam's far-flung diplomatic corps." Grew's children and grandchildren enjoyed the summers they spent at 19 Grew Drive and Birch Ridge and looked forward to the rare occasions when faraway relations could all be together in Hancock.

In his memoir, Grew recalls his career as a turbulent one. "The peaceful world of diplomacy that I knew in my early experience was shattered by two world wars…catapulted from a world of serenity into one of turbulence and distress." His posting to Japan proved the most challenging yet brought him the most public acclaim. Grew made the cover of *Time* magazine on November 12, 1934, because of his presence in Tokyo, "decidedly the hottest, the most crucial U.S. diplomatic post in the world." The article within documents the difficulty of Grew's position as relations between Japan and the United States steadily deteriorated, noting that he "did his best to check the ire of mounting tempers and to clear the way for intelligent, thoughtful negotiation." Following the attack on Pearl Harbor, Grew was forced to endure a harrowing interval of internment in Japan before returning to the United States with his family in 1941.

Grew devoted the rest of his career to educating the American people about Japan. In his speeches, he was always careful to distinguish between the positive qualities of the people he had lived among and the "military machine" that had brought the country into war with the United States. According to biographer Heinrichs, "Career diplomacy in the modern world provides few opportunities for greatness, but [Grew] had a moment of greatness when, in the midst of the fantasy and hatred of war, he presented a realistic and objective view of the Japanese enemy to prepare the public mind for peace and ultimate reconciliation. His essential concern was peace, both as a way and an end." Grew resigned from the State Department the day after the surrender of Japan, on August 15, 1945.

# Part II

# Running the Town and Getting Around

## "A Good and Sufficient Pound"

When we were kids growing up here in Hancock, my family had a couple of backyard horses. There weren't many people keeping horses in town then, and everyone knew us because Dad was a selectman. So whenever a stray horse turned up, the assumption would be that it was one of ours, and someone would helpfully put it back in our field. More than once we came home to find horses we'd never seen before in with ours; luckily, they all got along. Eventually, the owners would appear and claim their animals; once we had a couple of extra horses for several days before someone came from a summer camp in Bennington to retrieve them. By then, we'd grown quite attached to them, and it was hard to see them go.

Two hundred years ago, though, stray livestock were a much more serious problem. They would break into gardens and laboriously hand-cleared hayfields and destroy crops needed to sustain local families. So every town built a strong enclosure, usually of stone, known as the "Town Pound." Hancock apparently had two pounds, one built in 1785 in an unknown location and one built in 1794 on the site of the present parking lot for the town beach. The "new" pound was ten rods square (each side about forty feet long), had six-foot-high stone walls and was four feet thick at the base,

The town pound.

tapering to two feet thick at the top. There was a "good gate," lock and key. Jonathan Bailey bid off the building of the pound at the annual town meeting for fourteen dollars and two shillings. Daniel Morse was appointed pound keeper.

In 1791, the State of New Hampshire passed a law requiring all towns to provide "a good and sufficient pound...in some convenient place...for the impounding and restraining of all swine, cattle, sheep, or other creatures." Towns that failed to provide and maintain one of these structures would be fined for every year "that they shall be destitute of such a pound." The law also specified the various fees for catching and delivering the different types of livestock to the pound, keeping them there and returning them to their owner.

The process of claiming stray animals was almost as elaborate as the fee structure for impounding them. If the owner could be determined—usually through a characteristic "ear mark" unique to each livestock owner and registered with the town—then he was contacted and could reclaim his animal after reimbursing the town for the expense of catching, impounding and keeping it. If the owner was unknown, a public notice had to be posted in Hancock and in two adjoining towns. If an owner still failed to appear, the person who impounded the animal was entitled to take it home, with the understanding that the legal owner could reclaim it within a year by reimbursing the town and the person housing it for all charges and expenses. If the person who brought the animal to the pound didn't want it, it was sold at public auction.

Should an owner or anyone else try to avoid paying fees by removing livestock from the pound "without lawful authority," the punishment was severe. Either they paid a five-pound fine in addition to the cost of reimbursement or they were subject to sixty days' imprisonment or "whipping, not exceeding thirty stripes," at the discretion of the New Hampshire Court.

Eventually, it became easier to keep livestock fenced, and strays became less of a problem. Pounds were abandoned or thriftily disassembled for their component parts. The Hancock Historical Society has the only existing photograph of Hancock's town pound, taken before it was dismantled in 1889. The stones were hauled across the Common and incorporated into the foundation of the newly moved and remodeled Center School, previously the Baptist Scientific and Literary Institution, currently the Town Office Building.

## Up the Hill to the Poor Farm

In 1834, the residents of Hancock purchased an old farm in the north part of town to be used as a "house of correction for the keeping, correcting and setting to work of rogues, vagabonds, common beggars, lewd, idle and disorderly persons." Despite the language taken directly from the New Hampshire statutes, there is no record of a criminal element in Hancock requiring incarceration at that time. The town simply intended to house its poor on the farm. There they would be cared for in a way that "would be calculated to discourage indolence and intemperance,—two fruitful sources of pauperism." The purchase of a town poor farm was in keeping with the prevailing climate of social reform; the poor were blamed for their own troubles. Communities hoped that putting the able-bodied to work on a farm would "reform" them so that they might once again become productive citizens. At the same time, they could help provide for those who weren't able to contribute to their own support, thus lowering the expense of public relief for the town's taxpayers.

Prior to purchasing a town pauper farm, Hancock had relied on a patchwork system of "outdoor relief" for its poor, providing the use of a cow, fuel or foodstuffs for families in need or auctioning off the annual support of orphan children and paupers at the town meeting. The lowest bidder

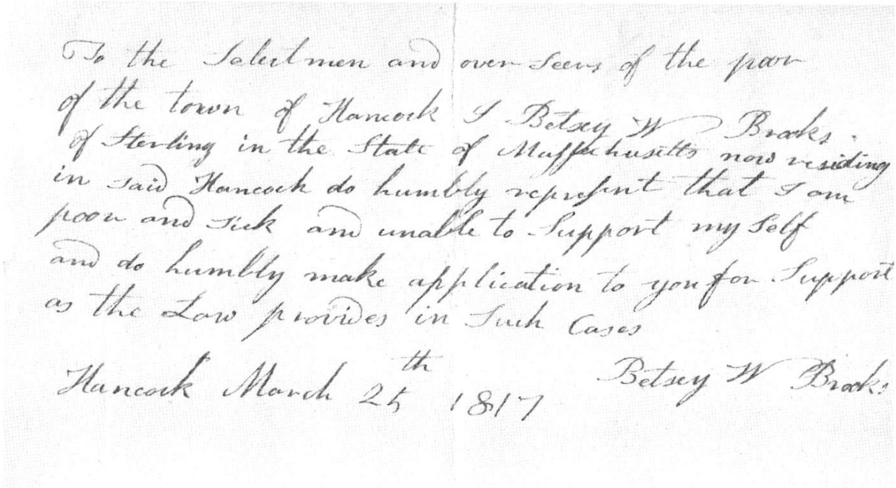

To the Selectmen and over Seers of the poor
of the town of Hancock I Betsey W Brooks
of Sterling in the State of Massachusetts now residing
in said Hancock do humbly represent that I am
poor and sick and unable to Support my Self
and do humbly make application to you for Support
as the Law provides in Such Cases

Hancock March 25th 1817 Betsey W Brooks

Betsey W. Brooks's 1817 application for town support. "I am poor and sick and unable to support myself."

promised to shelter, clothe and feed these individuals at the least expense to the town, in exchange for whatever work the pauper might be able to contribute to their household. At best, this was a practice that humiliated those whose difficult circumstances made it impossible for them to care for themselves; at worst, it led to the abuse and mistreatment of a community's most vulnerable citizens. The town hoped to avoid the worst ills of the earlier system by housing the poor together in the care of a couple hired and supervised by Hancock's overseers of the poor.

The Hancock town poor farm continued to operate as a working farm and poorhouse for almost twenty years before it was sold in the 1850s. At that point, the town returned to its earlier practices of poor relief or sent paupers to the county poorhouse in Hillsborough. The only extant record of the town poor farm is a slim, leather-bound account book that combines everyday farm accounts with brief and poignant references to Hancock's poor.

A page recording the delivery of cattle to pasture in 1845, for example, also notes that the "Kyes family came to Pauper Farm Sept. 18, 1851 seven in number"; a child of this family subsequently died. The account book records the visit of the local doctor and the purchase of the young boy's coffin. Another page records the twenty days neighbor Elbridge Burtt spent haying on the farm, as well as the arrival of a new resident. "Mrs. Abigail Allen came to Pauper Farm Oct. 14, 1849 with nothing except her wearing apparel." Abigail's sister, Lorena Hills, on the other hand, is recorded as having brought with her in 1844 a chest of drawers, a bedstead, an array of bed linens, a feather bed and a straw tick. Near this careful inventory of personal belongings is an undated note: "sow pigd."

The stories of Hancock's paupers and their experiences on the town poor farm are difficult to extricate from the historical record. The very fact of their poverty renders them almost invisible, as they seldom owned property or paid taxes and tended to be laid in unmarked graves. The town poor farm is also long gone, as is the small neighborhood of farms that surrounded it on Nahor Hill, located at the end of North Road where it intersects with High Street. Its legacy is the important role it played in Hancock's long struggle to cope with the burden of looking after friends and neighbors who could no longer take care of themselves.

## All Aboard for Hancock

It is hard for us to imagine the excitement that greeted the first steam locomotive through Hancock in 1878. The railroad had been a viable and desirable form of transportation since the 1840s; for years Hancock and neighboring towns lobbied hard for railway service to their communities. The railroad lines that reached Keene, Nashua, Hillsborough and even Peterborough by 1871 connected those fortunate towns to Boston, New York and points beyond. Passengers to and from Hancock were still limited to travel by six-horse stage, and local farmers and manufacturers depended on horse-drawn wagons to laboriously cart their goods to rail stations in other towns.

The biggest obstacle to connecting the rail lines from Keene to Nashua through Hancock was, of course, the ruggedness of the terrain. The route required an enormous investment in cutting and filling, as well as the construction of elaborate trestles due to its steep grades and numerous ravines. The original contract estimated an expenditure of $46,500 per mile to build the rail bed, for a total cost of $1,200,000. The towns that would be served by the line had to commit to paying the railroad company a gratuity

The original wooden trestle over "Alcock's Ravine," between Stoddard and Old Dublin Roads.

consisting of 5 percent of their total valuation; Hancock had to pay about $17,000. It still took three years for the "Manchester & Keene" line to be completed, as the railroad struggled with insolvency and mismanagement. By contrast, the "Peterborough & Hillsborough" line cost only $18,000 per mile to build on the level plains along the Contoocook River.

The two lines opened within a month of each other in the summer of 1878. Hancock had three stations: the Hancock Depot just outside the village center on Depot Street, a small station on Cavender Road and, most notably, the "junction" at Elmwood, just off South Elmwood Road. Although the in-town depot was important to the citizens of Hancock, Elmwood Junction played a larger and far more important role in the regional rail system—it was here that the east–west and north–south railway lines intersected. The junction boasted an unusual feature known as a "wye" that allowed trains on either line to be transferred to the other line in either direction. There were also coal sheds for refueling, an elevated water tank, a house for the resident stationmaster and a very busy station, which even had its own post office.

By 1887, both lines were controlled by the Boston & Maine Railroad Company, with several regularly scheduled daily passenger and freight trains (including a regular milk train until 1925). Freight exported from Hancock included logs, lumber, clothespins, apples and livestock. The railroad also opened up the area to visitors and summer people; at times the Boston & Maine ran two extra daily passenger trains to accommodate summer travelers, some of whom would be met at Elmwood and others, at the depot in the center of town.

But train traffic to and from Hancock came to an abrupt end in the 1930s. After a trestle located between the depot and Longview Road washed out in 1934, the B&M Railroad discontinued the line from Keene, through Hancock village, to Elmwood. A devastating flood in 1936 ended rail service between Peterborough and Elmwood. Although the Hancock Depot was saved from destruction in the 1970s, the once numerous buildings and support structures of Elmwood were not so fortunate. A recent hike of the property, now owned by the Town of Hancock through the generosity of Dick and Eleanor Amidon, reveals very few traces of the bustling train station that once existed there.

## Building, Breaking, Rolling and Grading the Roads

Thanks to our hardworking town and state highway crews, it is easy today to take our well-maintained roads for granted. It was a far different story a few generations ago, as documented in Hancock's town records, stored in the town archives. In 1910, there were 2 automobiles and about 240 horses in town, and travel was mostly by horse-drawn wagon or carriage over gravel roads that varied greatly in construction and condition. Without a regular crew, Hancock's road agent depended each year on local residents to provide the manpower, teams and raw materials required to keep roads passable.

A snow roller and a six-horse hitch.

Every year, a significant portion of the annual budget went to men who used their own teams to "break" Hancock roads in the winter, dragging logs or simply relying on the force of their animals' bodies to open roads through heavy snow. Hancock didn't invest in a snow roller until 1904; this heavy, horse-drawn wooden roller packed the snow to make a smooth, hard surface for sleighs and other vehicles. The town also paid an individual each winter to "snow" Hancock's half of the covered bridge over the Contoocook River, ensuring a sufficient level of snow inside the bridge for sleighs to travel without interruption.

As noted in James and Donna-Belle Garvin's *On the Road North of Boston: New Hampshire Taverns and Turnpikes, 1700–1900*, during much of the year it was mud and deep ruts that rendered some New Hampshire roads nearly impassable. From earliest settlement, towns such as Hancock required every male resident to either work a certain number of hours building and maintaining local roads each year or else pay an additional "road tax." With little agreement regarding either method or material, local roads varied widely in composition and condition. Small streams and swampy areas were particularly vexing to early road builders; stone culverts worked well but were laborious and time-consuming to build and maintain. More often, they would simply sink logs and other debris in low areas until they could build a "surface" on top of them with rocks and gravel. Such routes could be as treacherous and unreliable as early bridges, known to collapse without warning and imperil the lives of unwary travelers.

In 1885, the town of Hancock took a big step, investing $250 in the latest technology, a "Thatcher Road Machine." Still in active use in 1910, this early grader drawn by multiple teams of horses or oxen dragged loose gravel from the edges of the road back to the middle, smoothing out wheel ruts and rough horse tracks along the way. This was apparently a vast improvement in efficiency and consistency over earlier methods using individual teams with plows, harrows and horse-drawn scoops.

According to the Garvins, it was the notoriously poor condition of New Hampshire roads that finally motivated state officials to assume responsibility for certain important routes during the second decade of the twentieth century. In addition to taking over the expense and maintenance of highways such as State Routes 137 and 123 in Hancock, officials made a concerted effort to improve travel conditions throughout the state. Bridges were rebuilt, and roads were paved to accommodate increased traffic by automobiles. Towns like Hancock invested precious resources in manpower and new equipment and adopted approved practices of road construction. The well-maintained paved and gravel roads we travel so easily today are the direct result of years of focused attention on the part of our community, heralded by the 1885 arrival, by train, of the Thatcher Road Machine.

## Moving the Highway: When the Neon Light Went Out in Hancock

A fragment of discontinued road is barely visible in the wetland alongside Route 202, just beyond the Daloz farm at the junction of Peterborough Road (Route 123), a remnant of the *old* State Route 202. This major north–south roadway once followed Peterborough Road into the center of town and Bennington Road from the fountain back out to the Bennington line.

A dramatic increase in traffic on New Hampshire highways, beginning in the prosperous years following World War II, contributed to a booming tourist business in scenic New England villages like Hancock. Joe Quinn, farmer and lifelong Hancock resident, owned the "Village Farm," the large, white colonial house and attached barns at the corner of Main Street and Bennington Road. In 1946, he and his wife built the one-story building that still stands at the base of Norway Hill Road to offer takeout ice cream, homemade pies, sandwiches and grilled items, in addition to seasonal vegetables, fruit and cider. They later added a fireplace-warmed room with booths at the rear of the building so diners could enjoy their food inside. A neon sign proclaiming "Snack Shop" could be seen all the way down Main Street. By the mid-1950s, however, the increased traffic was taking its toll on New Hampshire's highways, and the state embarked on an ambitious project to upgrade its major thoroughfares. This effort was applauded by the communities along these routes, and in July 1956 Quinn volunteered to serve as part of the Hancock delegation to the Route 202 Association.

The state initially presented several proposed alternatives to upgrade Hancock's section of the highway. Two options involved creating a "by-pass" to divert the route from the center of the village, either by following the route of the discontinued rail line along the river, four miles away, or via a "wilderness route," only two miles away but running through territory deemed "heavily wooded and remote" between the Peterborough and Bennington town lines. The proposed routes through the village involved the sacrifice of historic homes and local businesses. One choice diverted the highway to School Street. Another maintained the original route but required the destruction of the large building next to the gas station housing Hancock's only industry, the "Hancock Tool Company," along with all the homes on the east side of Bennington Road, beginning with the "Village Farm." A third option proposed an underpass at the foot of Norway Hill. Unwilling to force an unpopular decision on the town, the state invited input from Hancock residents; a hearing on the matter was held in early 1957.

By the date of the hearing, the state had conducted additional research, and the available options were reduced to two: the in-town route that would destroy homes and businesses along Bennington Road or the wilderness by-pass route. But Quinn came prepared to the hearing with a *third* option, designed by his son, Dick, an engineering student at Villanova. This route preserved the historic village center by directing the highway over the top of the then sparsely populated Norway Hill. This was the option greeted most enthusiastically by those attending the meeting—a compromise for those concerned that the important thoroughfare should be "kept in close" for the sake of local businesses and those who wanted it moved outside of the village to preserve Hancock's historic New England character. Unfortunately, Quinn's Norway Hill option was ultimately rejected by state officials due to the severe grade of the proposed route. At the town meeting of March 1957, the ballot vote was 160 to 20 in favor of the bypass. Construction began the following year.

According to Dick, the Quinn family was very disappointed in the decision to move Route 202 away from the center of Hancock. After a few years, they closed their popular restaurant and extinguished Hancock's first and only neon sign, although Joe continued to sell seasonal produce and make cider in the barn at the Village Farm through the 1970s. Generations of Hancock youth were thrilled to see Joe's whimsical, life-sized, stuffed oxen reappear each year to herald the advent of pumpkin season; sales of the popular vegetable averaged five hundred per year in the 1960s.

Newspaper accounts of the protracted decision process resulting in the relocation of Route 202 from the center of Hancock to its outskirts reveal how wrenching the experience was for its citizens, striving to preserve both the special character of their village center and its economic vitality. According to the *Peterborough Transcript*, there was real fear that diverting the well-traveled highway would cause the small community of six hundred residents to fade away. When presented with final plans for the bypass in late 1958, one selectman asked the state "if it would erect signs on the by-pass to let motorists know that Hancock still exists."

## "Direct Popular Government in its Purest Form"

The hotly contested 2008 presidential primary brought an unprecedented number of Hancock voters to the polls. Yet this wasn't the first time Hancock voters turned out in record numbers to participate in the political process. On Tuesday, March 8, 1960, a record 329 "citizens and spectators" crowded the town hall (on the first floor of the meetinghouse) to vote for the presidential candidate of their choice, cast their ballots for local officials

*From left:* Cynthia Kinney, Antonius Speekenbrink of the Netherlands and Selectwoman Bessie Bradley.

and debate twenty-nine warrant articles at the annual town meeting. Of particular interest that year was the presence of foreign observers: students from Turkey, Korea, Thailand, Tunisia, Liberia, Japan, Pakistan, the Netherlands, Antilles, Israel and Brazil, visiting from the Fletcher School of Law and Diplomacy in Medford, Massachusetts. Brought to Hancock by the United States Information Service, these young people hoped to "witness the functioning of direct popular government in its purest form."

A comprehensive photographic record of the day is housed in the archives at the Hancock Historical Society; there are amusing images of folks making their way to the meeting along paths lined with shoulder-high snowbanks (and not one political sign in sight). The most contentious issue at the town meeting that year was whether Hancock should adopt zoning regulations;

the vote was 111 to 99 against zoning. The foreign visitors were apparently most amused by the debate concerning whether the Hancock Highway Department should plow private driveways; voters decided overwhelmingly in favor of continuing the practice. Moderator Karl Upton led the meeting, accompanied by Selectmen Tom Kierstead, Bess Bradley and Ernest Adams. A heavily laden table of baked goods and coffee staffed by cheerful women provided sustenance for those who participated in the daylong event.

The polls closed at 6:00 p.m.; the only local race was a contest for road agent. Everett Adams was reelected over Clarence Hanson, 155 to 113; 195 of Hancock's 210 Republicans voted for Richard Nixon, and 29 of the 43 local Democrats voted for John F. Kennedy. A weary Daniel Devins, town clerk, closed the long, eventful day by calling in the final poll results to county officials and the press at 10:30 p.m.

It was the unusual presence of foreign observers at an archetypal New England town meeting that inspired an unknown photographer to snap so many pictures on that early March day forty-eight years ago. Yet in his carefully composed photographs he documented far more than just one politically significant day in a small town in a quaint and picturesque region of America. He also unknowingly captured and preserved for us forever images of that most cherished aspect of every Hancock town meeting and voting day: the dearly familiar faces of friends and neighbors coming together to decide our town's—and sometimes our nation's—future.

## Looking Out for One Another: Twelve Years as a Selectman

In 1962, Dick Amidon started his first term as a Hancock selectman, an office he held until 1974, when he resigned to become town moderator. The selectmen met every Monday night in their office on the first floor of the meetinghouse (now the office of the First Congregational Church), adjoining the town hall. As the town has changed over the years (there were fewer than eight hundred residents in 1962), so have the duties and responsibilities of the selectmen.

In the 1960s it was the selectmen who appraised all the property in town for tax purposes; each spring they visited places where changes or additions had

A 1960s town meeting. *From left*: Selectmen Bob Strombeck and Dick Amidon, Burt Manning, Charles Adams, Bill Brown and Lesley Wright. *Courtesy of Dick and Eleanor Amidon.*

been made. They followed state guidelines for valuing property and made comparisons based on recent real estate transactions. (When asked how they knew if a property was modified or changed hands, Amidon replied that "everyone knew.") In addition to appraising the real estate, the selectmen also had to count the number of livestock and fowl on each property to be taxed as personal property. Values were assigned to animals according to formulas provided by the state. Amidon notes that it was an unwritten rule among the selectmen that once a man died, his property never increased in value for the rest of his widow's life. "It was one of the ways people in town looked out for each other."

Along with valuing each resident's property, the selectmen also had to count the number of "polls," adults eighteen years of age and older, each of whom was required to pay an annual poll tax of ten dollars. This was a town tax levied to defray the cost of running elections, holding town meetings and more. It was the selectmen's duty to ascertain whether the adults at each residence were to be "booked" to Hancock or if they legally resided somewhere else. Amidon particularly remembers one woman's response when they asked her if a certain man still resided at her home: "You can book him in Hell, for all I care."

Each section of Hancock's boundary line had to be walked ("run") once every seven years by the selectmen or their representative, in company with a selectman or representative from the adjoining town. According to Amidon, the most difficult section was the boundary with Antrim in the vicinity of Willard Pond and Route 123 North, as the line was particularly complicated and the terrain was very steep. It was the responsibility of the selectmen to make sure that the boundaries between towns were maintained and the legal maps updated.

One of the least savory aspects of a selectman's duties in the 1960s was the payment of bounties on wildlife deemed "noxious pests" by the State of New Hampshire. At any time, a selectman could find himself receiving an unexpected visit from someone bearing the heads of dead porcupines, each of which was worth fifty cents. For well over one hundred years, New Hampshire selectmen had been required to pay bounties to local residents providing evidence that they'd killed bears, wolves, bobcats or certain other species of wildlife determined to pose a risk to local agriculture. Generations of young men had found the practice a ready source of extra cash; one longtime Hancock resident remembers when the bounty on two porcupine heads equaled the cost of a six-pack of beer. It was up to the selectman dispensing the reward to dispose of the remains to prevent someone from collecting more than one bounty payment for the same animal.

Reflecting on his experiences as a selectman, over thirty-five years ago, Amidon remembers how informally the town operated then, relying on mutual cooperation to get things done. For instance, when the picket fence surrounding Norway Plain Cemetery needed replacement, local resident Willis Johnson came up with the idea of stringing heavy chain between the granite posts as a low-cost, long-lasting solution to the problem. Amidon provided the chain and a six-pack of beer, Johnson provided the bolts and together they built the fence that stands there today. And when the selectmen's office was moved from the meetinghouse to the old high school on School Street, the selectmen cleaned, painted and furnished their new room themselves, at no cost to the town.

The selectmen no longer personally deliver town reports from door to door, and today they enjoy the welcome assistance of a capable town administrator. Still, Amidon considers the selectman's job much harder now than it used to be, porcupine heads notwithstanding. His many stories and fond recollections of his years as a selectman remind us that the spirit of community we value in Hancock today is due in no small part to those who have volunteered to serve over the years—and who served so well.

# Part III

# Special Events and Milestones

## "Keeping Old Home Day"

By the closing decades of the nineteenth century, rural northern New England was in decline. The best and brightest of its native sons and daughters were fleeing rocky farms for better opportunities elsewhere, and long-settled family homesteads were being abandoned at a frightening rate. Communities like Hancock looked back with nostalgia to the days of their founding, viewing life back then as simpler and more rewarding. Inspired by the town's centennial celebration in 1879, descendants of one of Hancock's founding families began holding an annual reunion of family and friends each August in Hancock. By 1886, this gathering had evolved to include members of the entire community and was known as the Symonds Reunion and Hancock Town Picnic.

When New Hampshire governor Frank Rollins instituted statewide observance of "Old Home Week" in 1889, Hancock simply incorporated the "new" holiday into the one already established, ensuring the continuation of what has become Hancock's most beloved and enduring summer tradition. Governor Rollins hoped to capitalize on the widespread nostalgia for a "golden, olden time" by luring successful natives back to celebrate, and help revitalize, their hometowns. The annual event certainly proved popular in

A 1961 Old Home Day parade float, with Hancock Little League team. *Courtesy of Paul Daly.*

Hancock; former residents and friends streamed back into town each August to "keep Old Home Day."

The 1907 celebration was typical: a band concert and a ball game pitting Hancock players against a team from a neighboring community kicked off the day, followed by a picnic lunch in "Goodhue Grove" on the shores of Norway Pond. The official ceremony followed in the afternoon, held in the meetinghouse sanctuary made festive with evergreens and ferns, bouquets of goldenrod, golden glow and other bright yellow flowers. The local minister offered the invocation on the gathering, and both residents and visitors shared prepared addresses, special poems, musical entertainment and reminiscences. Later, everyone had the opportunity to visit the "historical rooms" or tour one of Hancock's oldest homes; a second ball game concluded the day.

As the years progressed, Hancock's Old Home Day festivities evolved. An evening dance in the town hall proved popular, as did the addition of water sports and an "aquatic ballet," mounted drills by equestrians from Sargent Camp, livestock exhibitions by area 4-H members and, beginning in 1937, a parade. This soon became the most anticipated event of the celebration; in 1954, the Old Home Day parade boasted an astonishing thirty-five floats entered by families and local organizations. For many years, the grand marshals led the procession on horseback, accompanied by a band and an impressive contingent of participants from local summer camps, veterans, fire equipment, livestock and children on decorated bicycles, in addition to the popular floats. Along with the parade, an ice cream social on Friday evening, a 5K road race and a fire department chicken barbecue have become Old Home Day mainstays.

The success of Hancock's Old Home Day tradition depends now, as it always has, on dedicated volunteers supported by a high level of community participation. Old Home Day is when we both celebrate and proudly display the community spirit that continues to make Hancock a special place to grow up in, to live in and to come back to, every third weekend in August.

## Turning on the Lights

On July 18, 1921, the citizens of Hancock celebrated the arrival of electricity in town with a gala celebration at the town hall. The Peterborough band, local schoolchildren and ninety girls from Sargent Camp provided musical entertainment; more than three thousand people attended the evening ceremony, which culminated in the first-ever lighting of Main Street and the Common.

At the annual town meeting in March 1921, Hancock had voted to borrow about $10,000 to purchase the materials and hire workers to construct the necessary infrastructure of poles and wires that would bring electricity to downtown Hancock. The Keene Gas & Electric Company supervised the project and supplied the power; by making use of existing poles erected by New England Telephone & Telegraph in 1904 they were able to electrify the center of town relatively quickly. The goal for the first year was forty customers; forty-eight households were successfully electrified.

A committee of three local residents managed the construction and maintenance of the system; every year the committee published a detailed report of its progress in the town report. Employing a construction company, local labor and teams of horses, the committee extended the lines an average of three to eight miles per year at town expense, adding seven to twenty households each year to their list of customers. Some routes were more challenging than others, due to "hard digging and excessive trimming," and there were still residents in outlying parts of town waiting for power ten years after the initial electrification of the village. In 1931, Hancock entered into a contract with Public Service of New Hampshire to supply the town's power, although the community retained ownership of the poles and responsibility for the construction and maintenance of the lines for several more years.

For the citizens of Hancock, electric light was not only a welcome replacement for cumbersome oil lamps but also a source of wonder. In December 1921, Fogg's Store (now the Hancock Market) enchanted

William Titus and his home at 11 Main Street. Note absence of electric wires and the old streetlight.

everyone with a holiday display featuring a Christmas tree decorated with tiny electric lights, the first ever seen in town.

## Grace Coolidge Star of Sesquicentennial Celebration

In the archives at the Hancock Historical Society, there is an old photograph of a family reunion, probably taken at the home of (Warner) Clark Goodhue on 84 Antrim Road (now the home of Hunt and Sara Dowse) in 1908. The reigning patriarch, Benjamin Goodhue, is proudly seated at the center of his large family, but one's eye is immediately drawn to a young woman with large and luminous dark eyes seated near the front of the group. This is Goodhue's granddaughter, Grace, who five years earlier had married an up-and-coming lawyer and politician in Massachusetts named (John) Calvin Coolidge Jr.

Long a prominent name in Hancock, the Goodhue family first arrived in town from Antrim about 1790. Grace's father, Andrew J. Goodhue, born in 1848, was the fourth generation of Goodhues to make their home in Hancock. Andrew went to Nashua to learn the trade of machinist, married Lemira Barrett of Merrimack and initially settled in Hancock, but shortly thereafter he moved with his wife to Burlington, Vermont, to take a job with a steamship line on Lake Champlain. Their only daughter, Grace, was born in Burlington. Following her education at the University of Vermont, Grace moved to Northampton, Massachusetts, to learn how to teach the deaf. It was there where she met her future husband, the man whose political career would thrust her into the public eye as first lady of Massachusetts and then as the wife of the thirtieth president of the United States following the sudden death of Warren G. Harding in 1923.

As a child, Grace made frequent visits to her grandparents' home in Hancock, at the corner of Main Street and Forest Road (currently the home of Gary and Shelly Merrifield). There she played with other local children, some of whom she was delighted to see again when she returned to Hancock after a twenty-year absence to help the town celebrate its 150th birthday, or sesquicentennial, on Old Home Day in 1929. The highlight of an extravaganza referred to as "the greatest celebration in the town's history,"

The sesquicentennial flag-raising ceremony. *From left*: Frank Stearns, former attorney general John Sargent, New Hampshire governor Charles Tobey, Grace Coolidge, Foster Stearns and an unidentified military aide.

local and Boston newspapers described Coolidge's visit in minute detail. According to the August 22 issue of the *Peterborough Transcript*, Coolidge left the bedside of her ill mother in Northampton, Massachusetts, to return to Hancock for the event. She stayed at the home of family friends Mr. and Mrs. Foster Stearns, who lived in Worcester, Massachusetts, but spent their summers at the Whitcomb House on Main Street, now the home of Tim and Emma Lord. Stearns was the son of Boston department store magnate Frank Stearns, Calvin Coolidge's friend and major benefactor.

From the beginning of her visit, Coolidge charmed everyone present with her friendliness and gracious manner. Refusing to ride down Main Street in a formal procession, Coolidge instead made her way along the sidewalk by foot, shaking hands and smiling as she acknowledged old friends. Once she arrived at the reviewing stand, she fascinated the crowd by bringing forth a newfangled "pocket" motion picture camera, which she used to record the parade as it passed by.

As part of the festivities, Coolidge and the other dignitaries present, including New Hampshire governor Charles W. Tobey and retired U.S. attorney general John G. Sargent, participated in a special ceremony to dedicate the flagpole that still adorns our Common, a gift of Mr. and Mrs. Stearns to the town in honor of its $150^{th}$ birthday. According to the August 23 issue of the *Boston Post*, Coolidge herself raised the first flag, while the band played and an airplane "swooped down from the sky and circled about."

The *Post* reported that ten thousand people came to Hancock to celebrate its sesquicentennial, many drawn by the celebrity of Mrs. Coolidge and her husband, who had also tentatively accepted an invitation to attend the gathering but then did not appear. The paper referred to Hancock as "a town that time has touched but never changed"; by 1929, the town had only six hundred residents and had a reputation as a "summer community" for those who spent the rest of the year elsewhere.

Although small in number, the people of Hancock were apparently enthusiastic and hardworking, with a dedicated corps of talented volunteers who went all-out for its big birthday celebration. The event featured a lengthy parade, stunts by visiting aviators, band concerts, water sports and many other activities. Culminating the celebration were two performances of a grand, outdoor pageant of Hancock history, called *The Homing Way*; fully one-third of the town's population had a role in the production. Coolidge's final, official act was to plant a commemorative tree on the Common in front of the school (now the Town Office Building); Governor Tobey planted one as well. Then she left town to return to her home in Northampton.

The Hancock Historical Society has several artifacts and documents that serve as visual reminders of this special day in our town's history, including the shovel Coolidge used to plant the tree. But the historical record makes it clear that the most cherished souvenir of the day for many local residents was the memory of the visit by the gracious and warmhearted former first lady, whom they still proudly considered "one of their own." Margaret Perry, president of the Old Home Day Committee that organized and hosted the sesquicentennial celebration, had the pleasure of presenting Grace Coolidge and other attendant dignitaries to the gathered crowd on that special day. Noting first that "Hancock is one of the smaller towns of New Hampshire, and we are doubly proud to have with us today such distinguished friends and well-wishers," she went on to introduce Coolidge as one "who comes from an old and honored Hancock family…we know her people through and through, and it has not surprised us to see how naturally and inevitably she has won the respect, the love, and the deep sympathy of a nation. And how easily she has won them—simply by being—herself!"

## NEW HAMPSHIRE CRAFTS ON DISPLAY—1935

Many Hancock residents eagerly anticipate traveling to the annual League of New Hampshire Craftsmen's Fair, held for a week each August at the Mount Sunapee Resort in Newbury, New Hampshire. In 1935, however, the second annual league fair came to Hancock. For five full days, hundreds of visitors thronged the village to attend demonstrations by craftspeople, special historical exhibits and daily dramatic presentations and to purchase the finest examples of traditional New Hampshire crafts.

Although today we take the presence of talented artisans in our communities for granted, at the turn of the twentieth century there was a real fear that some traditional skills were going to disappear altogether. People who had practiced crafts such as fine woodworking, glass blowing, hand-weaving and ironworking for generations were dying out. At the same time, young people were abandoning rural New Hampshire in droves for better economic opportunities in more urban areas.

The Colonial Revival and Arts and Crafts movements of the late nineteenth and early twentieth centuries idealized traditional forms of handwork and inspired a national revival of interest in them in the 1920s and 1930s. People started to seek out isolated craftspeople in rural areas to purchase examples of finely crafted decorative items for their homes and to learn these "forgotten" skills. Handcrafts associated with New England's colonial days were particularly valued as representative of America's idealized rural and "simpler" past.

The League of New Hampshire Craftsmen was established in 1932 to preserve and promote the tradition of fine handcrafts in the state of New

"Hancock Home Industries" league shop, located at 59 Main Street.

Hampshire through education and by providing a market for the products of rural craftspeople. According to league literature, the village of Hancock, "widely known for its beautiful shady main street, its fine church and old doorways and fences," was deemed an ideal location for the organization's second annual celebration of traditional crafts and the people who created them. One of the league's statewide shops, known as Hancock Home Industries, was located at various times at 18 Main Street, 27 Main Street (Moller's) and the Grange Hall (59 Main Street). Mrs. Foster W. Stearns was an avid needleworker who managed the shop and was instrumental in bringing the 1935 fair to Hancock.

The hugely successful, weeklong event attracted a large crowd to Hancock to purchase baskets, textiles, glass, jewelry, pottery, metalwork and furniture, all "products of New Hampshire labor and New Hampshire materials." The town hall, Vestry and horse sheds housed the main exhibition's craftspeople and articles for sale, with special historical exhibits at the library and at the historical society building. A luncheon was available at the Grange Hall (now the post office). Each afternoon, county representatives of the Rural Recreational Extension Service presented elaborately staged dramatic productions on the theme of "America's Heritage in the Arts," utilizing the natural amphitheatre behind the horse sheds. The final and culminating presentation featured a "Greek ship, bearing a dozen beautiful dancers which wafted across the waters of Norway Lake to ground on the sandy beach before the audience." In its account of the fair, the *Peterborough Transcript* reported that "native New Hampshire ingenuity and resourcefulness was never better exemplified than at Hancock this week."

## A Fast Ride in the Dark

"Two or three people would sit on the toboggan, you'd get your feet all together, start down that chute in the light and then you were plunged into darkness, going like a shot down into the valley. Just after you caught your breath there was a right angle turn into the field. Why we didn't kill ourselves, I don't know." In 1935, when Hancock native Karl Upton was a member of the town's Outing Club, the group constructed a toboggan chute that ran from Main Street down through the ravine to Old Hancock Road and the valley beyond. According to Upton, Sime Sheldon, then managing the local gas station at the corner of Peterborough Road and Main Street, strung a wire across the road to light a single bulb on a pole at the start of the run. But after that, it was a fast ride in the dark.

Hancock had a very active Outing Club in the 1930s, hosting a variety of community events year round. According to the February 7, 1935 edition of the *Peterborough Transcript*, the toboggan chute was merely one attraction of many featured at that year's Mid-Winter Carnival, sponsored by the club. The weekend event also included ski races down the side of a mostly treeless Norway Hill, snowshoe races and hockey games. A Carnival Ball was held at the town hall on Saturday night, and "fancy skating" and a wood-chopping contest rounded out the activities on Sunday. The toboggan chute and skating rink were open to the public all weekend long.

A 1935 toboggan chute running from Main Street into the valley.

But the exhilarating toboggan ride was just one form of winter sledding once popular in Hancock. Old-timers also love to talk about the moonlit nights when young people would gather with their double-runner sleds on the top of Norway Hill and coast down the snow-covered road into the village. Upton, whose memories of growing up in Hancock were recorded at a historical society program in 1986, remembered the average "run" for a sled starting at the orchard to have been about halfway down Main Street. He did admit that there were those who claimed to have coasted all the way down Main Street to the bottom of Sand Hill (Route 137 S) before stopping, one of them being Mildred Weston, a spirited young woman who eventually became his wife. "If she did [make it all the way to the bottom of Sand Hill], I'm sure she was exceeding the speed limit."

When asked about the wisdom of sledding on public highways in the dark, Upton shrugged off the danger, responding that in the village at night there was "very little traffic" and that "there weren't any lights that amounted to anything anyway." But while conceding that "there were no broken bones," he didn't make light of the peril inherent in a ride down that infamous toboggan chute. "I'm not very proud I did something so foolish as that—it was really dangerous the way that we went."

## When Santa Came to Town

The first Hancock "Town Christmas Party" was held in the town hall (the first floor of the meetinghouse) on December 20, 1952. The sponsoring committee consisted of the presidents of all the town organizations, and the entertainment was provided by the children of the Hancock Elementary School. By all accounts, the event was a huge success. "Everybody in the community showed up," reported the *Peterborough Transcript*, describing the "large audience" that greeted the arrival of "Santa," bearing candy and gifts for the children. Thus began one of Hancock's most beloved and enduring holiday traditions, carefully documented in a small notebook kept for that purpose and stored at the Hancock Town Office Building.

In 1953, it was decided to make the town Christmas party an annual event, with a committee consisting of a delegate from each town organization: the fire department, Grange, PTA, Sewing Circle, Sportsman's Club, Guild, Men's Club, Woman's Club and the Congregational Church. Each group also contributed five dollars toward the purchase of candy, popcorn, oranges and small trinkets to be distributed to the children, as well as a "gift" for Santa (initially cigarettes; in later years a box of candy). Within a few years, other town organizations had joined the fun: the Boy Scouts were putting up the tree and the Girl Scouts were decorating it.

Eventually, the responsibility for hosting the annual event was turned over to individual organizations, with each group participating in turn. The Hancock Preschool and the historical society became involved, and the fire department's Ladies Auxiliary was pressed into service one memorable year to fill in for the men of the fire department, called away to fight a fire at Sargent Camp. There were also a few years when inclement weather caused last-minute cancellations and required heroic rescheduling efforts on the part of sponsoring organizations and school staff to ensure that the popular event would still be held.

From the 1950s through the mid-1990s, as many as 150 Hancock children eagerly participated in each year's festive celebration and were thrilled at the arrival of Santa—so memorably portrayed over the years by Hancock residents Al Daloz, Bruce Skinner, Mert Knowles, Francis Pond, Norm Phelps, Joe Rasmussen, Chris Streeter and Bob Fogg. Christmas trees were generously donated each year by the Merrions of Hilltop Farm and the Lohmillers of Find-Us-Farm. In 1987, the party was moved to the sanctuary on the second floor of the meetinghouse to better accommodate the growing crowd.

But in 1996, the staff of the Hancock Elementary School requested that the town hold its celebration separately from the school's annual Christmas concert, and attendance began to plummet. Since then, despite the best efforts of local organizations and loyal supporters, the town Christmas Party has struggled to survive. By 2004, the number of participating children had dwindled to twenty-three. Finally, the town was forced to make the difficult decision to discontinue this longstanding, local tradition, known for so many years as "the annual Christmas party which everybody in Hancock attends."

## Into the Snowy Woods

Fifty years ago, unusually heavy snowstorms in February and March added so much snow to what was already on the ground that one Hancock resident claimed that "the squirrels were halfway up the trees before they started to climb." A group of folks defining themselves as "mature citizens" were inspired by the plentitude of snow to revive an older winter tradition; they started the Hancock Snowshoe Club.

Community snowshoe hikes were popular in New England in the late 1920s and 1930s. Usually beginning just after Christmas, young and old alike would don their heavy woolen outerwear, gather up their wooden and rawhide snowshoes and meet at a prearranged spot in anticipation of a delightful outing in the winter woods.

Longtime New Hampshire state senator Bob English was an enthusiastic member of the Hancock Snowshoe Club; he and as many as forty others would meet at 11:00 a.m. on a winter Saturday morning, with sandwiches in their pockets and the promise of hot coffee at their destination, to explore Hancock's snow-covered "old trails and wood roads." English documented their exploits in his annual review of community happenings, printed in each year's town report. For more than a decade, these popular outings continued, but by the early 1970s, cross-country skiing was starting to replace snowshoeing as the winter sport of choice. Some claim that it was the advent of the snowmobile that put an end to the quiet enjoyment of the woods on snowshoes.

From the late 1950s through the early 1970s, the Hancock Snowshoe Club provided a welcome social outlet and opportunity for pleasant outdoor exercise during the short days of late winter and early spring. The 1874 song of the "Montreal Snow Shoe Club," as recorded in *The Snowshoe Book*, written by William Osgood and Leslie Hurley, certainly would have resonated with this active group:

*If the strength and glory*
*Of youth you would recall,*
*Then exercise your lungs and limbs*
*On snow shoes with our call*

# Part IV

# Disease and Disaster

## Stranded by the Blizzard of 1888

The unusually large snowfalls of recent years remind us that this region has always been subject to extreme weather conditions, especially in the winter. Although today our efficient highway crews typically have roads cleared in a matter of hours, one hundred years ago it was a different story. Clearing roads and railway lines of snow could take days.

One particularly memorable snowstorm was the Blizzard of 1888, which fell in March of that year and wreaked havoc with the transportation systems of the day. Ella A. Robinson lived on her family's farm at Elmwood Junction, a busy train station at the intersection of two major railway lines located just off South Elmwood Road and Route 202 in Hancock. In addition to marketing the produce of their farm, during the railroad's heyday Ella's family provided food and lodging for railroad officials, workers and travelers. In the published history of Hancock, *The Second Hundred Years of Hancock, New Hampshire*, Ella shares her memories of the 1888 storm and its aftermath:

> *A trainload of people was stranded at the house during the great blizzard of 1888. The last trains to reach Elmwood on the twelfth of March were stalled there for four days. The passengers and train crews were marooned.*

Elmwood Junction and the Robinson farm, before fields were flooded to create Powdermill Pond.

> [My family] *prepared supper for thirty-five people that night. Those who could not be lodged in the house slept in the barn. In these days of easy access to markets, no house would have been so well stocked with provisions.* [We] *were then milking seventeen cows and making seventy-five pounds of butter a week. The cellar was filled with potatoes, vegetables, apples and cider. Besides poultry and eggs,* [we] *had on hand a side of beef and a dressed pig. The men brought in wood and kept the fires going and helped the women with the housework and cooking. There was only one woman among the guests. They made biscuits by the peck and cooked other things in proportion. They beguiled the hours while the storm raged and the snow drifted to the tops of the windows with much singing, card playing and impromptu entertainment. Each person contributed his specialty. There was a minister and a lawyer in the company besides the popular lecturer, George Makepeace Towle, who delivered the lecture that he was scheduled to give in Concord at that time.* [Towle was a politician, historian and author who contributed regularly to *Harper's Magazine*.]

Although the railroad station at Elmwood is long gone, the Robinson homestead remains in the family, as it has since 1807. Much of the original pastureland and meadow now lie under Powdermill Pond, but the family still enjoys vacationing at the old farmhouse. Ella's youngest daughter, Elizabeth (Terrill) Wheeler, recently died at the age of 101. As a child, Betty enjoyed the hustle and bustle of the busy train station and once recalled that when she went to Hancock Village as a young girl she "found it very quiet and she was always glad to get back to Elmwood where there was something exciting going on."

## "At Home on a Spanish Vacation": The 1918 Influenza Epidemic

The year 1918 found Hancock, as it did much of the rest of the country, preoccupied with the war then raging in Europe. Every available resource was targeted to that purpose and every local paper filled with patriotic exhortations. But in late September, news of another sort began to appear in the *Peterborough Transcript.* Local citizens were falling ill in great number to a fast-moving sickness with flulike symptoms, vaguely referred to as "the

A "winter auto" used by local doctors to travel on unbroken roads during "flu time."

Spanish Grippe." Twenty-nine residents of Peterborough alone had already become ill, most of whom were children. By October 3, the first local deaths were being reported.

The first person in Hancock to die from complications of this terrifying new form of influenza was a young woman named Florence Sturtevant. According to the *Transcript*, Miss Sturtevant had been out of town working in Massachusetts at the onset of her illness; according to the Hancock vital records, she was also pregnant. Like the recent, modern outbreak of swine flu, the 1918 influenza epidemic was unusual in that although people of all ages caught the virus, it was healthy young adults who most typically died from it. And pregnant women were especially at risk. Sturtevant was an otherwise healthy twenty-six-year-old who became ill and died three days later. Her son, who must have been delivered at the onset of the illness, lingered on for an additional twelve days before he, too, succumbed.

A few days later, it was one of Hancock's young servicemen who died: William Henry Robinson, whose family lived at Elmwood. Robinson was stationed at Camp Grant in Illinois, where he became ill while awaiting deployment overseas. Five thousand young soldiers sickened with the virus at Camp Grant; five hundred died, including young Robinson. Although it was in these crowded military bases that "the virus reached first and with most lethality," according to John Barry's 2004 *The Great Influenza: The Epic Story of the Deadliest Plague in History*, Camp Grant achieved further notoriety because of the actions of its overzealous commanding officer.

Confident that newly implemented gauze masks would be sufficient to control the spread of the virulent illness, Colonel Charles Hagadorn deliberately ignored new army regulations on overcrowding designed to help arrest the progress of the influenza virus. The consequences for his soldiers and staff were devastating; the news that more than one hundred young men and women had died at the base on a single October day drove Hagadorn to take his own life the following afternoon.

Not everyone who contracted the virus died. In New Hampshire, roughly 10 percent of those sickened with influenza developed the complications that led to death by pneumonia a few days later. Week after week, the Hancock correspondent for the *Transcript* listed those who were ill, wryly noting on October 10 that one local woman had left her Claremont teaching post to recover at home in Hancock: "Ellen Weston is at home on a Spanish vacation." A week later, he gratefully wrote that there was still "considerable sickness in town but all are reported improving." In a letter home to his folks in Hancock, quoted in an unpublished memoir by his daughter Anna Mary Adams Wallace, young soldier Charles E. Adams reported that he had been hospitalized for ten days with influenza while serving in France but was on the mend. Sadly, his neighbor and occasional employer, thirty-seven-year-old farmer and apple grower Charles Vatcher, would be struck down by the virus the following January.

But while individuals and families in Hancock and surrounding towns struggled to cope with the mysterious illness and the loss of young lives, the virus was also wreaking havoc on community life. The October 3 issue of the *Transcript* prominently featured a plea from the chairman of the New Hampshire Committee on Public Safety, John Jameson, written in light of the recent flu outbreak, which appeared to be "a serious menace to health and life in our state." Jameson recommended that "theatres, moving picture houses, schools, and other places where people congregate indoors be temporarily closed…and that people do not attend public meetings or travel in railroad trains except as is necessary." Citizens were also reminded that, despite the frightening epidemic, the war still remained everyone's primary concern. "It is true now…due to the war conditions, that there is a very great scarcity of nurses and physicians. So that anyone, who employs a nurse unnecessarily for their comfort or convenience, is open to severe criticism, and no nurse worthy of the name should accept such hire." Rather than call a physician, people were advised to get plenty of fresh air, eat well and rest and to prevent the spread of the disease by staying home. They were also warned to beware the "safe, sure, and harmless" remedies advertised by manufacturers of patent medicines, quick to prey on the fears of those who felt helpless against thc relentless epidemic.

According to Barry, influenza outbreaks are typically characterized by an initially rapid spread of the virus, soon checked as populations develop an immunity to it. In 1918, it usually took only six to eight weeks from the first case in a community to the end of a local epidemic. That certainly seemed to be the case in Hancock and much of New Hampshire, most affected from the end of September through early November. By October 24, the ban on public gatherings had been lifted, churches resumed and schools reopened. On October 28, the epidemic was considered to be at an end.

The Hancock correspondent to the *Transcript* gratefully reported in the October 31 issue that, once again, "Hancock found itself settled pleasantly into the old order of things." Yet the epidemic had taken quite a toll. Just in the month of October 1918, Peterborough had lost ten to influenza and Concord had lost one hundred. Hancock lost four: the two Sturtevants, "our splendid young hero" Robinson and Charles Fellows, a sixty-year-old farmer. And local residents continued to die from the illness and its effects months later; twenty-two-year-old Fred Hill died the following January, along with Vatcher. The final death recorded in Hancock due to the illness was a baby born on April 3, 1919, Ralph Ernest Richardson, whose death three days later was attributed to "trauma from influenza."

## ROBBED OF OUR TREES: THE HURRICANE OF 1938

Seventy years ago, a powerful ocean storm veered suddenly and unexpectedly in a northwesterly direction, carving a path of death and destruction across coastal and central New England. Luckily, no lives were lost in Hancock, and there was minimal structural damage. But the torrential rain and driving winds that lashed the community that September day terrified local residents and drastically altered the local landscape. In Hancock, the Hurricane of 1938 is most remembered for what it did to the trees.

By 1938, many Hancock farm pastures had already been abandoned to forest. These pasture trees, mostly white pines of similar age and girth, fell most readily to the storm's violent winds. The pines that fringed the shores of Norway Pond also went down, as did many of the majestic maples that lined Main Street, heaved from the sodden ground as the ferocious wind found purchase in their leafy crowns. The damage was sporadic throughout town, depending on a tree's age, species and where it stood. A single specimen in a forest might be broken in two or an entire stand laid flat. Many trees stood denuded of all their branches and leaves. In some parts of town, it was estimated that 80 percent of the standing timber was blown down or uprooted. Total board feet of pine, hemlock, spruce and hardwoods destroyed in Hancock was estimated in the millions.

Within days, a hastily created government agency, the Northeast Timber Salvage Administration, responded to the crisis. Residents who had lost valuable timber stands would be compensated for saw logs of specific dimensions delivered to designated holding sites in each community. Water storage facilities were recommended to keep the logs in useable condition longer, guaranteeing the best resale market. In Hancock, the logs were brought to Nubanusit Lake and Norway Pond.

Officials stationed at the lakes received hundreds of logs, assessed their value and arranged for payment. Landowners had to retrieve and haul the wood—no easy task given the obstructive slash and debris in the forests and the limited tools and technology available. Even the twenty lumbermen brought in to clear the acres of downed timber on the "island" between Lakes Nubanusit and Spoonwood had only axes, crosscut saws and horsepower. On Nubanusit, they constructed a "boom" or log corral to limit harvested logs to one section of the lake; residents remember intrepid youths walking across the tightly packed logs without getting wet. On Norway Pond the following summer, bathers were warned to stay away from the free-floating debris.

Eventually, most of the wood was milled into lumber at newly constructed sawmills and sold, although many logs sank and remain visible on the lake bottoms today. Local men welcomed the opportunity to earn extra money

Norway Pond, serving as a holding site for logs from trees downed in 1938 hurricane.

clearing roads and town property, and WPA workers were brought in to help. Firewood was so plentiful the following year that local farmer John Welch felt lucky to get six dollars per cord for each of the estimated one hundred cords he had cut and split, if he could sell it at all.

For one Hancock farm family, though, the sudden loss of their carefully tended timber stand to the hurricane precipitated a unique crisis. For years they had counted on the profits generated from the harvest of their wood to send their only child to college. When little Anna Mary Adams had arrived for her first day at the Hancock school, the teachers put her in first grade with all the other children her age. But on her second day of school, they decided to move her ahead to the second grade; on the third day, they finally figured out that this bright little six-year-old belonged in the third grade, where everyone else was two years older.

By the time Anna Mary was ready to graduate from Hancock High School in 1946, it was clear that this talented young woman deserved to continue her education. Her graduating class certainly thought so; they voted her in the top 5 percent of seniors most likely to succeed. But by then the family woodlot was gone, sacrificed to the hurricane, and the low profits realized from the sale of salvage timber were too little to make her college dreams come true. So Anna Mary took a chance and entered a nationwide Pepsi-Cola college scholarship competition—and won. Four years of college at the institution of her choice for a bright young farmer's daughter born and raised in a tiny New Hampshire town.

Anna Mary Adams Wallace completed her college education at the College of Wooster, in Wooster, Ohio, went on to get a graduate degree, married and settled down to raise her own children in Chicago. But her family still owns the farm on Middle Hancock Road, which they return to as often as they can. As is true throughout Hancock, the devastation wrought by the Hurricane of 1938 is no longer evident on their lovely property, where the beautiful trees stand tall once again.

## THE FOREST ABLAZE

In late April 1941, a spark from a portable sawmill in Marlow set off a massive fire that burned for three days, ultimately destroying 24,000 acres of forest and farmland and many homes in Marlow, Stoddard, Gilsum and Washington. The Great Marlow Fire, as it is remembered, is still considered the worst forest fire in New Hampshire history. But there was another fire burning at the same time, one that consumed 2,500 acres in Hancock, Nelson and Harrisville. Kindled in a sawdust pile at the Nelson end of Tenney Pond, just to the east of Lake Nubanusit, the second blaze threatened homes and farms on the Old Dublin and Jaquith Roads and along King's Highway. In the village, the skies were darkened, and ashes rained down as helpless homeowners anxiously watched the progress of the two simultaneous conflagrations.

Three years earlier, the Hurricane of 1938 had damaged or destroyed hundreds of acres of trees in the Monadnock region. As part of the local recovery effort, portable sawmills were set up throughout the damaged woodlands to salvage whatever downed timber was still deemed marketable. Three years later, the woods, littered with enormous piles of sawdust, deadfalls and brush, were a veritable tinderbox after an open winter and dry spring. All it took was a spark to ignite a fire that moved so quickly that, according to longtime resident Karl Upton, it raced up the slopes of

An early 1900s view of Mount Skatutakee from Norway Hill.

Skatutakee and the Thumb, over the ridge and down again in one afternoon. At one point, the exhausted firefighters thought they had put it out, but the wind started up again and reignited the blaze, which raged on.

Every able-bodied man in Hancock and volunteers from miles around joined together to fight the fire, including every boy from Hancock High School. Howard Weston remembers fighting the fire as a young teen, along with Bill Hanson and Bill Weston Jr. Bill Weston, his father, and family friends Merle Jones and son took turns perching high on the roof of Jones's barn on Jaquith Road, now the home of Steve and Tricia Frohling. Every time a live ember landed on the wooden shingles around them, they doused it with a bucket of water, saving the barn and one farmer's livelihood as other firefighters worked to protect the house and garage. According to the *Transcript*, at one point the Jones property was completely surrounded by the blaze. After fighting the Hancock fire all day, Bill Weston Sr.'s daughter, Sarah Hutchins, remembers that he spent the night helping the reported one thousand firefighters trying to turn back the massive Marlow fire, barreling east over Pitcher Mountain toward Stoddard village and Hancock beyond. That fire posed the biggest threat to the extensive Weston acreage and farms, located on the western edge of Hancock.

According to Wayne Fisher, local expert on the evolving technology employed by area highway and fire departments, the only equipment available in Hancock to fight the 1941 fire was a single, converted dump truck with a front-mounted pump and hand tools. All they could do was try to stop the progress of the onrushing blaze by chopping and digging firebreaks, mostly by hand. Sarah recalls that at one point a local fireman, H. Thorn King, came to the door and urged her mother to evacuate the family's Weston Road home to save herself and her children. Although anxious, Mrs. Weston knew that if they were in real danger, her husband would come and take them to safety, so she refused to leave. Hancock fire chief Ernest L. Adams did move his extended family from their home on Depot Road to safety in neighboring Antrim for the duration, according to his grandson, Bud Adams.

Directly in the path of the Hancock fire were several estates owned by wealthy, socially prominent Bostonians who had bought hundreds of acres on and near the mountains of Skatutakee and Juggernaut. Their remodeled farmhouses and cottages were popular summer destinations for their many friends and relatives. A few, such as Margaret Perry, daughter of the acclaimed impressionist painter Lilla Cabot Perry, made Hancock their home year-round; she maintained a herd of prized cattle at her family's Flagstones farm on King's Highway. According to the *Peterborough Transcript*, Miss Perry evacuated her valuable cows to protect them from the flames; Howard Weston remembers that she then came to stay with his family on School Street, stashing her mother's valuable paintings in their basement to keep them safe from the fire.

Despite the unfolding dramas in the hills outside of town, Hancock children were apparently still expected to go to school. Sarah remembers how black the sky was as the ashes fell in the village, and the children were told to patrol the schoolyard for live embers during recess. When they returned to their classrooms, their clothing was black with soot.

It ultimately took firemen from Hancock, Hillsborough, Bennington, Francestown, Milford, Nashua, Wilton, New Boston, Antrim and Peterborough; three hundred members of the Civilian Conservation Corps camp at Warner; and "hundreds of volunteers" to put out the fire in the Hancock/Harrisville/Nelson triangle. Miraculously, no lives were lost and no homes destroyed. As reported in the *Transcript* on May 2, three days after the fire began: "This town settled wearily but gratefully into the ordinary ways of life yesterday after the fire on Skatutakee Mountain, worst in the memory of the people, was reported all out at 3 in the morning, and the one that came from Marlow…was reported to have veered away from Hancock."

# Part V

# The Civil War

## Abolitionist Fervor Divides Hancock

By 1860, the citizens of Hancock seemed to have been united in their belief that the inhuman institution of slavery should be abolished by whatever means necessary, including war. But twenty years earlier, when abolitionist fervor was first building and infiltrating even the most rural of New England communities, the message had a mixed reception. When prominent abolitionists staged a three-day antislavery convention in the Hancock meetinghouse in 1842, they and their supporters were met with ministerial denunciation, community derision and violence.

By 1840, Hancock residents were well acquainted with the evils of slavery. Until his death in 1826, a former slave known as "Old Jack," reputedly kind-hearted and beloved by all who knew him, had made his home in Hancock. The tale of his childhood abduction in Africa, when a white man "picked them up and carried them off just like a hawk would a hen," was well known; his tombstone in the Pine Ridge Cemetery was erected by voluntary contributions "in commemoration of his virtues."

Regardless of their personal sympathies, the majority of Hancock residents still looked to prominent clergymen to guide the community's response to issues of social concern such as those presented by the impassioned,

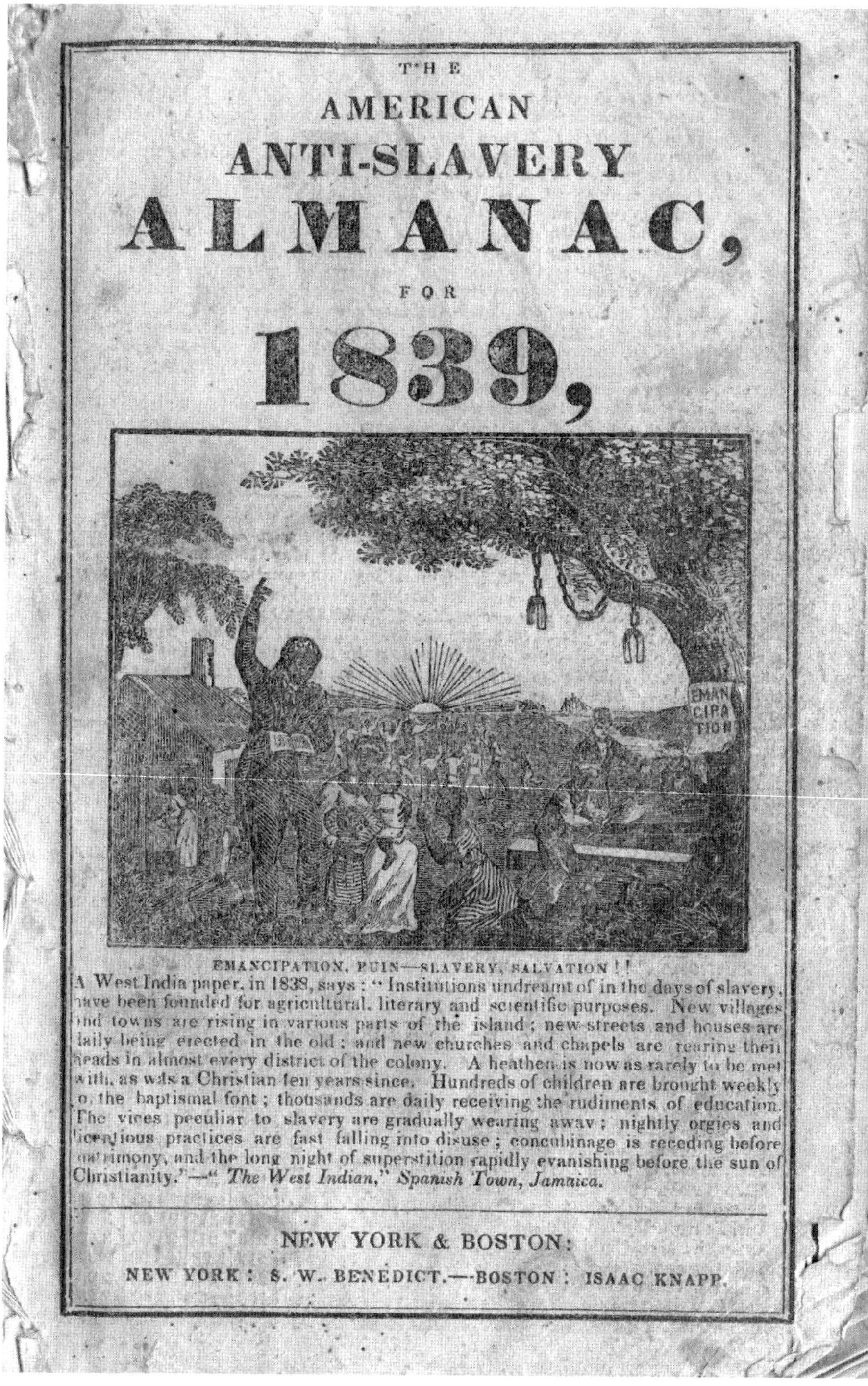

THE

AMERICAN

ANTI-SLAVERY

ALMANAC,

FOR

1839,



EMANCIPATION, RUIN—SLAVERY, SALVATION!!

A West India paper, in 1838, says: "Institutions undreamt of in the days of slavery, have been founded for agricultural, literary and scientific purposes. New villages and towns are rising in various parts of the island; new streets and houses are daily being erected in the old; and new churches and chapels are rearing their heads in almost every district of the colony. A heathen is now as rarely to be met with, as was a Christian ten years since. Hundreds of children are brought weekly to the baptismal font; thousands are daily receiving the rudiments of education. The vices peculiar to slavery are gradually wearing away; nightly orgies and licentious practices are fast falling into disuse; concubinage is receding before matrimony, and the long night of superstition rapidly evanishing before the sun of Christianity."—"*The West Indian,*" *Spanish Town, Jamaica.*

NEW YORK & BOSTON:

NEW YORK: S. W. BENEDICT.—BOSTON: ISAAC KNAPP.

The 1839 *American Anti-Slavery Almanac.*

early abolitionists. In Hancock, it was the well-entrenched Congregational minister Reverend Archibald Burgess who led the denunciation against the three prominent abolitionists in charge of the convention and those who dared attend it. Considered too controversial and inflammatory in both their message and means of transmitting it, the abolitionists persisted in continuing their Hancock convention to its official conclusion, despite low turnout and carefully orchestrated disruptions on the part of local youth.

The details of the event, pointedly absent from the local historical record, are documented in a contemporary issue of the abolitionist newspaper, the *Herald of Freedom.* According to those present, the disruptors progressed over the course of the meeting from noisy disturbance to hurling stones, shattering the windows of the meetinghouse. Fear of personal injury apparently did not deter an audience deemed "goodly, but not full"; it included students from both the Baptist Literary and Scientific Institution (original occupants of the current Town Office Building) and the Congregational Academy (located in the Vestry).

However contentious, the early abolitionists accurately predicted the outbreak of the Civil War, "a hand-to-hand conflict [that] must by and by come." Their Hancock supporters suffered religious excommunication and community sanction in the years before the abolition movement gained wide acceptance; some risked even more by actively aiding runaway slaves leaving Peterborough as part of the "underground railroad." Local historian Hayward wrote of one prominent early Hancock abolitionist: "The crowning joy of his later years was to witness the entire extinction of slavery and a unanimity of feeling upon a subject that for years was the cause of a bitter controversy."

## A "Thoroughly Modern" Antebellum Community

In 1860, Hancock was a bustling agricultural village boasting 844 residents. Sheep and cows far outnumbered people. Livestock grazed without care within a mostly treeless environment devoid of large predators since much of the local wildlife, including bear, wolves, deer and even beaver, had long since been hunted to localized extinction. Enormous flocks of passenger

An 1860s view of Cascade Farm on Old Dublin Road. *From left*: W.H. Weston, Alfred Barber, Clara Weston, Hattie Weston, George F. Weston and Elvina Weston. *Courtesy of the Weston family.*

pigeons still darkened the skies, but certain sites in town provided an ideal setting for nets used to ensnare these birds for local larders. Horses were necessary for local travel; the stagecoach transported travelers to area train stations for longer journeys. Townspeople could borrow books from the newly organized public library, housed along with the post office in one of the two general stores on Main Street. The Jefferson Inn (currently the John Hancock Inn) was a popular gathering place, although in 1860 Hancock was a "dry" town, thanks to the temperance reform movement of previous decades.

The abolition movement had contributed to a high level of antislavery sentiment in town; weekly publications such as the *Peterborough Transcript* provided a forum for public opinion, as well as a source of local and national news. Worshipers attended the Congregational Church in Hancock, which had outlasted attempts to establish Baptist, Methodist, Unitarian and Universalist religious organizations within the community. Children attended one of eight district schools, with the opportunity for education beyond the elementary level available (for a fee) at the Hancock Academy (located upstairs in the Vestry). The Hancock Literary & Scientific Institution (now Town Office Building) had closed a decade earlier, and a third "academy" had burned. Of the numerous mills and manufacturers that had once dotted Hancock streams, only a few saw- and gristmills and a single tannery remained. Most of the others were casualties of the environmental disruption precipitated by widespread land clearing in the early nineteenth century.

By 1860, though, most Hancock residents enjoyed the "modern convenience" of heating and cooking with cast-iron stoves instead of fireplaces, although there was still no running water and outhouses were a necessity. By the standards of the day, Hancock residents considered themselves thoroughly modern citizens, the fortunate inheritors of a model, and seemingly indissoluble, republic.

## Off to War: A Hancock Soldier Leaves Home

When twenty-year-old Edwin Ware left his father's farm to join the newly formed Company G, Thirteenth Regiment, New Hampshire Volunteers, in the summer of 1862, he was a local hero. Whether motivated by patriotism, a longing for adventure or by the recently instituted $100 enlistment "bounty," Edwin and the eight other Hancock men who responded to the North's call for soldiers that August were the pride of their families and community.

Despite a potentially disqualifying "malformation of the ankles," Edwin successfully passed obligatory medical examinations and was accepted into the regiment. After a few weeks of drilling in Peterborough, the new recruits departed for further training at Camp Colby, located on Concord's "heights." Edwin described his exciting journey in a letter written home to his family on September 14:

> *We left Bennington a little past 8, had to get out and march through the street, stop and listen to several short speeches, then we had a collation of cheeses, crackers, apples & cider. We had 10 teams to take us to the Cars* [the nearest railroad station, in Hillsborough], *where we arrived about noon. Then the boys piled in and we arrived at Concord Depot about ½ past 2. We then formed in lines and marched up street by the Office of the NH Patriot turned to the right and halted, at the Quartermasters*

A tintype of Edwin Ware taken while he was a soldier in the Civil War.

*situated at the east side of the bridge over the railway bridge. Here they gave us our housekeeping furniture consisting of a blanket, plate, tin cup, spoon, knife and fork, then they marched us west, about a mile to the Camp.*

In October, the Thirteenth Regiment left for Washington, from there to join the rest of the Northern army in Virginia. Once again they enjoyed a ceremonious departure, this time from Nashua. As reported by the October 11 issue of the *Peterborough Transcript*:

> [The Thirteenth Regiment] *marched to the Indian Head Hotel, escorted by the Nashua cadets and two engine companies, where they partook of a bountiful collation, prepared for them by the citizens of Nashua. After*

> *doing justice to the eatables, they again took up their march for the Worcester depot, and were soon on their way to Washington.*

The local paper proudly added, "[T]his regiment is well officered, and contains an excellent class of men...We shall hear good reports from them."

## Three Curious Herbs Shipped to Union Soldiers

Three curious herbs appear regularly on detailed inventories of barrels shipped to Union soldiers by the Hancock Soldiers' Aid Circle: hops, sage and wormwood. We know sage as a popular culinary seasoning, hops is important to the production of beer and wormwood is an interesting, if odoriferous, ornamental garden plant. But the fact that these three herbs were almost always included among items carefully selected to provide comfort to soldiers on the front implies that they were used differently in nineteenth-century New Hampshire and grants them a significance now forgotten.

Hops, sage and wormwood are perennial plants, hardy in Hancock and undoubtedly were a common feature of farmyard gardens in the nineteenth century. According to Mrs. M. Grieve, in her classic *A Modern Herbal*, all three have a long history of medicinal use. The female catkins of the vining hops plant, dried and sewn into a pillow (as on the barrel inventories) induce sleep, act as a sedative and are particularly helpful in relieving earache and toothache. The dried leaves of the sage plant, made into an infusion by steeping in boiling water, relieve mouth infections and sore throats; fresh leaves rubbed on teeth cleanse them and strengthen the gums. Externally, the infusion helps heal skin abrasions; its astringency aids in the care of more extensive wounds. Sweetened with sugar and lemon juice and taken as a "tea," the sage infusion was popular for relieving fever, stimulating digestion and promoting good health and energy as a "tonic." The bitter-smelling and bitter-tasting wormwood was also made into a popular tonic, although its most common use was to treat internal parasites and promote good digestion.

The number of those who perished in, or as a consequence of, Civil War battles was shockingly high. Yet easily twice as many soldiers died from disease during the conflict, due to inadequate diets, lack of personal hygiene and poor sanitation. Eager to improve conditions for loved ones so far away, the women of the Hancock Soldiers' Aid Circle worked together throughout the war, preparing and collecting items to be carefully packed in wooden barrels and sent to encamped soldiers. Drawing on generations of practical experience and rudimentary medical knowledge, local women contributed to the war effort in ways familiar and comforting to distant family members. Included among the warm socks and quilts were bandages and scraped lint for wound packing, vitamin-rich dried fruit and homemade jelly and traditional herbal remedies, all intended to help ease the discomfort of their boys on the front and hasten their healthy return to Hancock.

## A Soldier's Thanksgiving in 1863

"The box arrived last night…the goose was slightly specked with mold but I removed it and this morning carried it to Potts and he warmed it in his oven. I stewed some cranberries, Tom made some gravy…we had a good dinner." This is how Thanksgiving was celebrated by Hancock soldiers in the Thirteenth Regiment, New Hampshire Volunteers, stationed in Virginia in 1863.

The Civil War correspondence of Edwin Ware makes it clear that in Hancock, as in much of the rest of the nation in the mid-nineteenth century, Thanksgiving was the primary holiday of the year. A celebration of home and family, the event centered on a grand feast featuring the agricultural bounty of the preceding year. Dinner typically included not only the familiar turkey but also goose, pork, beef and chicken pie. Preparations went on for weeks and resulted in a staggering array of preserves, vegetables, breads and pies, among other accompaniments. A special church service preceded the meal, and family visiting, music, games and even formal balls concluded the festivities in the late afternoon and evening. Everyone who possibly could came home for Thanksgiving.

Edwin and his fellow soldiers, stranded far from Hancock, made do as best they could with holiday delicacies shipped in wooden barrels via train from loving families back home. "We have had a first rate dinner," wrote Edwin to his family in 1862, "one that we shall remember as long as we live with pleasure and the next one I hope to eat with you in old Hancock."

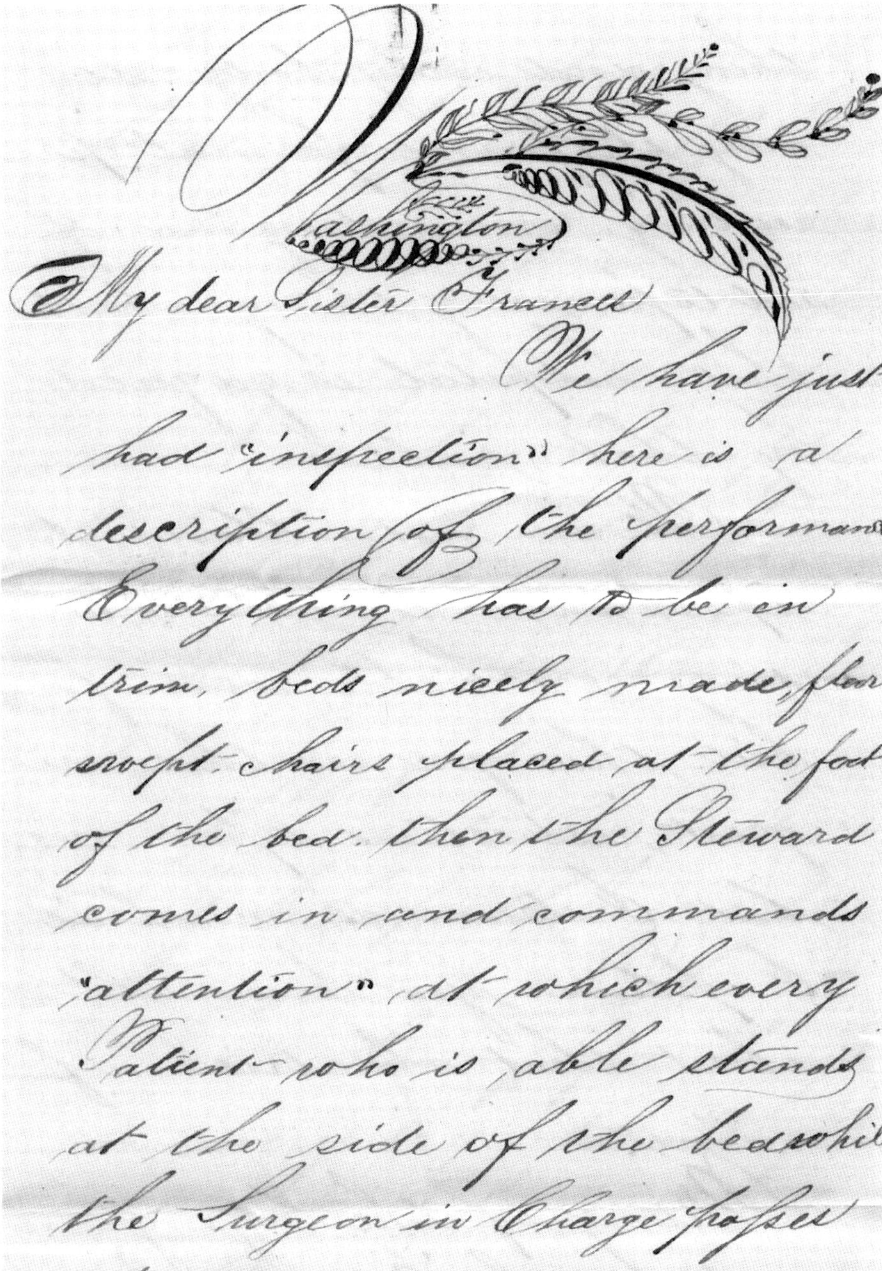

Washington

My dear Sister Frances

We have just had "inspection" here is a description of the performance. Everything has to be in trim, beds nicely made, floor swept. chairs placed at the foot of the bed. then the Steward comes in and commands "attention" at which every Patient who is able stands at the side of the bed while the Surgeon in Charge passes up and down viewing every-

An 1863 letter from Edwin Ware to his sister, Frances Ware of Hancock.

# THE DEATH OF MYRON TODD

Twenty-one-year-old Myron Todd of Hancock died in a makeshift hospital at Camp Bowers in Portsmouth, Virginia, in May 1863, one of the estimated 360,000 Union soldiers who perished during the Civil War, 17 percent of the total who enlisted. The families of these fallen soldiers were sustained in their grief by the nineteenth-century convictions that death was an unavoidable act of divine will, that families would reunite in heaven and that those who sacrificed their lives on behalf of the Union cause were fulfilling their national destiny. Myron's impromptu military funeral was described in a letter sent home by his boyhood friend Edwin Ware; both men were part of a group of seven from Hancock who enlisted together in Company G, Thirteenth Regiment, New Hampshire Volunteers in the fall of 1862.

According to *The Vacant Chair: The Northern Soldier Leaves Home* by Reid Mitchell, in the mid-nineteenth century death was still part of everyday life for most American families, as it had been for the generations preceding them. Infant mortality was very high, and death due to childbirth, accident or illness was all too common. Most Hancock residents, influenced by their Protestant religious heritage, probably looked on these tragic events as manifestations of divine will, "acts of Providence" that they could do little to influence or avoid. They took comfort, however, from a widespread perception of heaven as a place where loved ones would be reunited, and frequently referred to the act of dying as "going home." People found strength in identifying themselves as part of an extended, multigenerational family composed of both the living and the dead; this perception of life as part of a continuum was extended to include community and nation. Fallen soldiers had sacrificed their lives to fulfill the destinies of those who had predeceased them in pursuit of a common cause: the United States of America.

When Edwin Ware wrote home to describe Myron Todd's funeral, he knew that his firsthand account of this sad event would be shared with Myron's grieving family, anxious for reassurance that their son and brother had received a burial befitting the sacrifice of his young life. They no doubt took comfort from Edwin's assurance that, in addition to official remarks made on Myron's behalf, not one but two chaplains had performed the funeral service and offered prayers, "one of the most impressive and

Many of Hancock's Civil War soldiers are buried here, in Pine Ridge Cemetery.

solemn scenes I ever witnessed." He carefully detailed how the surviving members of the company marched alongside the ambulance carrying Myron's coffin, wearing full dress regalia and bearing arms out of respect for their fallen friend.

Edwin knew that families cherished the rituals of mourning, paying special attention to the selection of an appropriate final resting place for their loved one. He described the headboard erected over the grave as "a pine plank finished off and painted white…very prettily painted by some one in the Regt." Edwin added that, although Myron was "buried in the soldiers burying ground the date, no. of grave are taken so that he can be removed at any time." Myron's family might choose to have their son's remains brought home to Hancock, even as they looked forward to their future reunion with him in their spiritual home. After addressing the dispersal of Myron's personal effects, Edwin concludes his letter by revealing his own attitude toward death: "We do not know how soon our time will come but come it will and O! may we be found ready."

# Part VI

# Village Buildings and Institutions

## The *First* Meetinghouse

The First Congregational Church of Hancock takes pride in the classic, Federal-style meetinghouse it shares with the surrounding community. But did you know that this building, which dates in its current form from 1851, wasn't Hancock's first meetinghouse?

Even before the town was officially founded in 1779, the residents of Hancock had argued about where their all-important meetinghouse should be sited. They knew that the location of this building would designate the religious, municipal and commercial "center" of a community whose residents occupied farms as distant from each other as the shores of Lake Nubanusit and the far borders of Bennington (then part of Hancock).

Finally, in 1788, citizens voted to build the meetinghouse near the location of the current one, on "Norway Plain." They designed a simple post-and-beam structure forty-two feet wide, fifty-four feet long and twenty-five feet high, with "porches" or covered entryways at both ends. The materials needed to build the meetinghouse were bid off to local residents, with some contracting to contribute boards and others beams or roof shingles. Rye seed was collected to trade for the necessary nails and

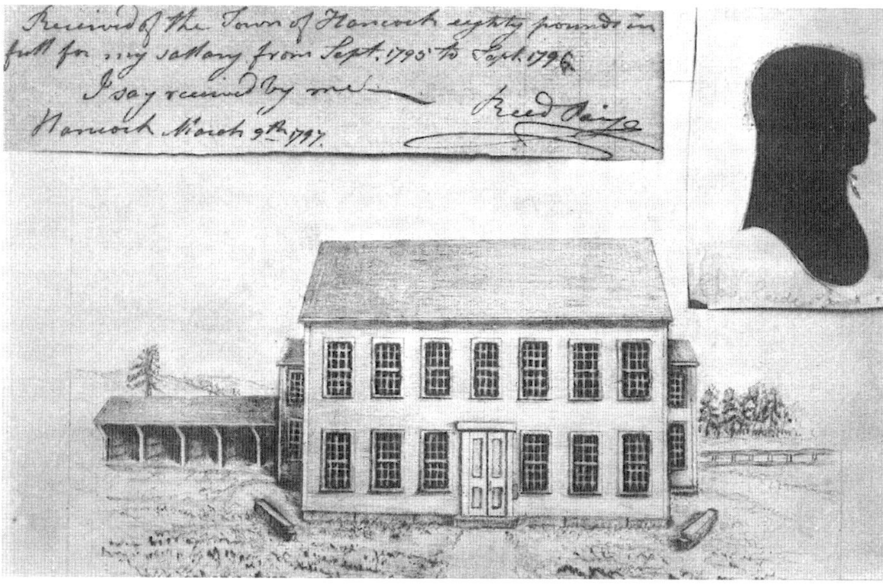


A sketch of first meetinghouse, with silhouette and signature of first minister, Reverend Reed Paige.

window glass since cash was scarce. The foundation was dug by hand and stones hauled to the site.

On the designated "raising day," in September 1789, fifty men gathered to raise the post-and-beam frame, with the help of several barrels of rum and beer. With the frame in place, it was yet another three years before the building was completely sheathed, roofed and plastered, as well as the pews installed. Nine years later, the exterior was finally painted; it was yellow, in the custom of the day, with the roof painted "Spanish Brown."

Sadly, after all the years of work and planning, a careless child carrying a coal from the blacksmith shop at the foot of Norway Hill to the schoolhouse across the Common apparently set the meetinghouse on fire; it burned to the ground in 1819. Only a few fragments of the original building are known to have survived; the Hancock Historical Society has two hand-carved floral ornaments that may once have adorned the pulpit.

## Historical Society Museum in Two-Hundred-Year-Old Tavern

In 1809, Joseph Symonds built the brick tavern building that now houses the Hancock Historical Society Museum, carefully siting the structure at the junction of what were then two well-traveled thoroughfares, Main Street and Bennington Road. Symonds had been running a tavern at his farm on Norway Hill since 1796; he hoped this new "public house," located in the center of the village, would attract enough business to support his recently married son, Charles.

Already a successful farmer, landowner and tavern keeper, the elder Symonds spared no expense in building the new tavern. At that time, it was one of the finest buildings in Hancock, built of local brick in the Federal style with a hipped roof and elegant interior detailing. The tavern boasted

A 1902 view of tavern building at 7 Main Street, now Hancock Historical Society Museum.

two parlors, two bedchambers, a ballroom and probably a bar and dining area, in addition to the spacious kitchen. A barn housed Charles's horses, oxen and cows, as well as the horses of visitors and travelers. The half acre of "tillage" and small orchard included on the property probably helped supply produce for the tavern table.

Five years after opening the tavern, however, Charles Symonds and his cousin, Henry Cummings, swapped both properties and livelihoods, with Symonds taking over Cummings's farm outside of town and Cummings moving to the village to run the tavern. In a letter home, John Boutelle, a contemporary of Symonds's, blamed this move on the economic downturn following the War of 1812: "As the times now are Charles has perhaps taken the most lucrative employment. Farmers suffer less by the present times than others."

Despite the poor economy, Cummings seems to have done pretty well running the tavern. Tax records indicate that he consistently carried \$80 to \$225 worth of "stock in trade" and owned one of the few carriages in town, in addition to his valuable building and real estate. But by 1828, Cummings, too, had given up on the tavern business, as well as on Hancock; shortly thereafter, he left town for New York State.

Hancock apparently had multiple taverns scattered throughout town, beginning as early as 1792. There were at least six in business at various times on or near Main Street, with as many as three of them operating concurrently. In the early nineteenth century, taverns weren't patronized only for meals, board and entertainment. Some local innkeepers were authorized to pay the town bounties for each dead crow or three blackbirds killed in Hancock between June 1 and July 1. Livestock traders advertised their presence on certain days to purchase "shipping horses." The owners of valuable stallions occasionally made them available at Hancock taverns for breeding local mares. And a visiting physician even advertised "Kine pox" vaccinations at one of the public houses on a May Saturday in 1803.

Eventually, the Symonds/Cummings tavern ceased operation as a public house. The building was subsequently owned by several individuals who used it as a rooming house and apartment building before it was purchased by the Hancock Historical Society for a museum in 1903. Although there have been some changes over time, Joseph Symonds's early attention to quality workmanship is still evident in this two-hundred-year-old building. Visitors can admire the old kitchen, the beautifully detailed woodwork in the front parlor and upstairs bedchamber and the original second-floor ballroom, extending the full width of the structure with matching fireplaces at either end.

## A New Meetinghouse Rises from the Ashes

After losing the first meetinghouse in a late October fire in 1819, the Town of Hancock and the "Congregational Society" moved quickly to replace their shared building. Much had changed in the small community in the thirty years since they had designed and constructed their first meetinghouse. Prosperous farms and small mills or "manufactories" now dotted the hills and streams of Hancock, and the village had a thriving commercial center, with stores, taverns and other businesses in addition to several fine homes. Local residents wanted their new meetinghouse to reflect their success, so they voted to design and build an elegant structure in the latest Federal style. Within a year, the new meetinghouse was finished; the dedication was held on October 25, 1820.

Built by Jacob Ames—the same local artisan who constructed the double-entry Whitcomb House down the street—the exterior of the new building was very similar to what we see today. It was patterned on earlier meetinghouses built in nearby Dublin (no longer standing) and Fitzwilliam; the designs of both of those structures had been inspired by a meetinghouse built in Templeton, Massachusetts, in 1811. Because of their strikingly similar architectural style and detailing, these four meetinghouses came to be known as the "Templeton Run."

But the new meetinghouse was sited well forward of where it is now, almost in the center of the Common area, and its interior layout was very different from the current configuration. The front doors probably led directly into a vestibule outside the ground-floor sanctuary, and there were balconies or "galleries" around three sides of the open interior. The pulpit was located on the fourth wall and was raised above the sectioned pews, each of which boasted its own numbered door. As in the earlier meetinghouse, these pew boxes were sold at auction, with the highest bidders vying for the most desirable seats. Meetinghouse pews were valuable "real estate," with subsequent changes in ownership traded as property and recorded in official deeds. Stylish and new, the Hancock meetinghouse was once again the proud center of its prosperous community. It would be *another* thirty years before the building was moved and dramatically reconfigured to become the familiar building that graces our historic district today.

## TOWN OFFICES IN FORMER BAPTIST ACADEMY

In 1836, the residents of Hancock voted to let representatives of area Baptist churches build a private secondary school on the Common. Ebenezer Ware built the two-and-a-half story Greek Revival academy building, with its gable end facing the center of the Common and serving as the entrance to the school. An early hand-drawn depiction in the archives of the Hancock Historical Society shows the same double-entry doors and pathways as the Congregational academy (Vestry) across the Common, built about the same time. The drawing also includes a small fenced yard with stiles to allow people to pass through but restrict access to the cows and other livestock that roamed freely through the center of the village and often grazed on the Common.

According to William W. Hayward's *History of Hancock, New Hampshire, 1764–1889*, the Hancock Literary & Scientific Institution opened in August 1837, with 152 male and female students. Although some students boarded with the Baptist minister (and academy instructor) Reverend Zebulon Jones in his home at 11 Main Street, others stayed at the Baptists' three-story Greek Revival boardinghouse across the Common (also built by Ebenezer Ware) or with local families. By 1839, the institution's annual "catalogue" notes that the academy boasted 342 students, of whom 104 were women and 71 were from Hancock. The majority of the scholars were from other New Hampshire towns, with several from Massachusetts and a few from New York State and Canada. Tuition was $3.50 to $4.00 per term, depending on the course of study, with additional charges for drawing, music and penmanship. Students unable to find room at the affiliated boardinghouse for $1.00 per week could find lodging elsewhere in town for $1.50 to $1.75 per week.

The annual academy catalogues indicate that students at the institution studied the classics, grammar, geography, arithmetic, "natural philosophy," chemistry, rhetoric, foreign languages and astronomy. There were laboratory facilities available, and every student attended a weekly Bible lesson, with the intention of "cultivating the feelings of the heart, as well as in disciplining the powers of the mind." Students participated in an active rhetorical society and contributed to the weekly school newspaper, the *Evening Star*, "devoted to literature, science, temperance, morality and the rights of man." Annual exhibitions, held in the meetinghouse across the Common, provided an opportunity for the students to display their knowledge, rhetorical skills and musical achievements. There were also field trips via horse and wagon to sights of local interest; a favorite activity was climbing Mount Monadnock.

By 1852, however, the religious organization in charge of the school, known as the "Baptist Church of Christ of Hancock and Society Land," had disbanded, "a majority of its members having either died or moved away." Hayward notes that the academy had closed a year earlier and that an attempt to revive it in 1858 failed. The building subsequently was used as a boardinghouse. In the late 1880s, the town voted to purchase the sadly derelict structure with the intention of converting it into a new village school, replacing the small, one-room brick schoolhouse originally sited nearby. In 1894, the building was moved onto a new foundation built of stones from the disassembled town pound and simultaneously reoriented so that its long side faced the Common. A new entry portico was part of its extensive remodeling in the Victorian style. Several generations of Hancock children attended elementary school in the former academy building before it was adapted once again to serve as the Hancock Town Office Building in 1997.

With the erection of a new elementary school a short distance away, the town of Hancock could have followed the lead of so many other communities, dismantling or dramatically remodeling this prominently located school that had served so many students for so many years. Instead, the town took advantage of its convenient location on the Common and adapted this beloved old building to serve a new purpose. Local residents and visitors still throng its administrative offices and popular meeting rooms five days a week, as did all those eager learners so many years ago.

## The Vestry, or "Hancock Academy"

In 1836, seventy men and women, members of the Congregational Church and Society of Hancock, each committed a certain number of five-dollar shares toward the construction of a "building which shall contain an apartment for the occasional public worship of God to be called the Vestry." The structure would also contain an "apartment for a public school and Academy." The original contract, now housed at the Hancock Historical Society, specifies that the building, with an estimated total cost of $1,000, should be constructed "as soon as convenient." There was no public school in Hancock at that time for students who had completed their educations at the nine elementary-level district schools; a two-story brick secondary school located somewhere near the meetinghouse (once attended by Franklin Pierce) had burned down in 1826. The town had an active Baptist congregation, however, and they were hard at work on their own "public academy"—the building that now houses Hancock's town offices, located across the Common from the meetinghouse.

The Vestry, or "Hancock Academy."

Both academies opened in August 1837. According to an advertisement in the *New Hampshire Sentinel*, "Hancock Academy, conducted by an association of Gentlemen, and kept in the large School Rooms over the Vestry of the Congregational Society" was intended for the "instruction of young gentlemen and ladies…in all those branches of Education necessary to qualify youth for the active duties of life, or young men for admission to College." It was also noted that "strict attention will be given to the moral and religious instruction of the pupils."

Reverend William Willis Hayward, in his *History of Hancock*, comments that the "spirit of rivalry" that undoubtedly existed between these two academies facing each other across Hancock's Common "was of incalculable advantage to the town." An early Hancock Academy catalogue lists the names of 297 students attending all or part of the year, many of whom were not Hancock residents but boarded here while pursuing their studies. The Baptist Academy also had more than 250 pupils during this time. Despite its early success, after six or seven years Hancock Academy briefly suspended operations and then opened only sporadically through the 1850s. The Baptist Academy had closed in 1851. Hancock students returned to the earlier system of individual tutoring by learned local residents or attended school and boarded in other communities.

Even though its school didn't endure, the Vestry's popularity as a site for both religious and community activities certainly did. Today the building is in almost daily use, hosting everything from watercolor painting classes to community suppers. In terms of the Vestry's value to the town of Hancock over the last 173 years, the initial five-dollar investments in 1836 brought a greater return than any of the seventy original contributors could have possibly imagined.

## A Meetinghouse Moved and Divided

In 1819, the State of New Hampshire passed what came to be known as the "Toleration Act." Towns could no longer tax every citizen to pay the salary of the local minister as they had since settlement; in effect this law "disestablished" the local Protestant clergy. Religious associations were allowed to form their own legal organizations and tax their members accordingly, for the support of their minister and their portion of the meetinghouse, if they had one. But it wasn't until 1850 that the citizens of Hancock voted to make the legal separation a physical one as well, by moving and remodeling their meetinghouse to provide separate areas for use by the town and the Congregational Society "so that the town and pew-holders might be better accommodated."

The meetinghouse was moved north from its location in the center of the Common so that the southern face lined up with the Vestry and other houses on Main Street. It was put on a permanent stone foundation, and the interior of the structure was rearranged. The partition wall that separated the entry foyer from the ground-floor sanctuary and meeting room was pushed back to just behind the second set of windows on the side of the meetinghouse. Beyond that point was the space to be occupied by the town for meetings and other uses; the town also retained the use of the small room under the stairs on the east side of the building for storing firewood to use in heating the new town hall. The "porch," entry and bell were to continue to be used jointly by both the town and the church. Later, a modification of the

A postcard image of meetinghouse and Vestry.

original plan resulted in the town lowering the floor of the town hall half a story during the moving and remodeling process, possibly to accommodate the stage.

The church was to remove the pews and raised pulpit and "erect all necessary supports for the floor above." Presumably this is when they drastically remodeled the sanctuary, building a new floor to raise it to the previous level of the upstairs gallery and erecting the current balcony on the north side of the room. They also probably reconstructed the pews at this time, abandoning the earlier boxed arrangement for the more contemporary layout that we see today. Except for the addition of the lower story on the back of the building, the exterior of the meetinghouse remained essentially unchanged. This explains the inconsistency between the location of the windows in the exterior walls and the internal layout of the structure in the area of the balcony.

Sadly, there is no written record to tell us just how they managed to accomplish such a massive undertaking. But it was this 1850 renovation that resulted in the current location and layout of the Hancock meetinghouse, familiar to all of us today yet vastly different from the 1820 original in its orientation to the rest of Main Street and the design and segregation of its interior space.

## The "Whitcomb Library"

The Hancock Town Library is composed of three separate structures: a 1925 Colonial Revival building facing Main Street; a clapboarded, contemporary addition at the rear; and, sandwiched between them, a small nineteenth-century brick structure with high windows. Today little more than a passageway between the two later and more substantial additions, this is actually what remains of Hancock's *first* library, built with great pride and opened to the public in 1882.

Hancock first established a public library for the benefit of its citizens in 1860, 150 years ago this year. For two decades, the steadily accumulating collection of books and periodicals was housed in the Tuttle Store, which used to be located between the present-day library and the double-entry Whitcomb House next door. The Whitcomb family—wealthy, educated and cultured—was very involved in ensuring the success of this popular

Whitcomb Library and Tuttle Store.

community institution, from the first 235 books purchased in 1860 through the construction of a dedicated building, and for many years thereafter.

John Whitcomb arrived in Hancock with his brother, Henry, in 1809. They soon established a very successful retail business and, within a few years, built one of Hancock's most elegant and expensive homes on Main Street. Beset by family tragedy throughout his adult life, Whitcomb nonetheless took advantage of every opportunity to educate his children and expose them to a variety of cultural opportunities, both here and in Boston. Only two of his five children survived young adulthood, one of whom, Adolphus, attended Harvard, received a degree in law and made a fortune handling the legal claims of miners during the California gold rush. Whitcomb's grandson, Adolphus D. Tuttle, was raised in his household following the untimely death of his young father and took over the family mercantile business upon Whitcomb's death in 1863. Tuttle was Hancock's first librarian, and it was to him that his wealthy uncle Adolphus sent word in 1880 that he would give the town of Hancock $2,000 if the town would agree to acquire "a piece of land as near the center of the village as can be obtained, and on said land erect…a brick building one story in height, with a tin or slate roof, to be called the 'Hancock Town Library Building.'"

The town of Hancock agreed to Whitcomb's stipulations and purchased a piece of land located on Main Street between the inn and the Tuttle Store, fifty-five feet wide and eighty feet deep, in a spot that "Interdum," Hancock correspondent to the *Peterborough Transcript*, described in July 1880 as "one of the best locations in the village—central and convenient of access." A plan was secured from "a draughtsman in Boston" for a twenty-two-and-a-half- by thirty-five-foot brick building, with twelve-foot walls, a slate roof and a "small annex for hall, wood room, etc." A year later, Interdum noted that the work on the new building was progressing well, thanks to skilled local craftsmen Alvah Copeland and Albert Jaquith, with the exterior walls finished and the roof ready for slate. In July 1882, the new library, "an ornament to our village," was completed and declared open for business. According to Interdum, there weren't any formal opening ceremonies because the "generous donor" was traveling in Europe. But he went on to describe the inside of the new building in great detail:

> *Two large rooms, one for a library room and one for a museum, have cabinets or cases on one side. The interior is richly finished in ash, with furniture, table, etc. of the same material. An elegant chandelier and eight bracket lamps light up the rooms; in the vestibule is a marble tablet with the following inscription: "Erected in memory of John Whitcomb by his son, A.C. Whitcomb, 1882."*

Not only did the library finally have its own building, its 1,350 books had also been "re-arranged and classified anew," and a fund had been established to ensure that the librarian would be able to "add from fifty to seventy-five books a year for all coming time." The total cost of the new library was reported as $4,306.35, of which Whitcomb had contributed $3,700.

Six years later, Whitcomb died, leaving the library another $10,000, as well as a second $10,000 to be used to beautify Hancock's bedraggled Common. According to longtime local historian and former librarian Doris Rogers, this generous $10,000 Whitcomb legacy, combined with two additional $1,000 bequests from Hancock natives Ebenezer Hubbard and Abijah Hadley, generated sufficient interest to cover all library expenses, salaries and the purchase of new books and periodicals throughout the remainder of the nineteenth century. In 1880, the town of Hancock voted unanimously "that in gratitude to the donor, and in appreciation of his respected father, John Whitcomb, Esquire, the building be hereafter known as 'The Whitcomb Library Building.'"

## "THE CHURCH INTERIOR...RENOVATED AND BEAUTIFIED"

At its annual meeting in March 1888, the Congregational Society of Hancock voted to celebrate its centennial with a grand renovation of the second floor of the meetinghouse. Preliminary plans were approved in May, the work began in June and the newly decorated church interior was revealed at the centennial celebration on August 28, 1888. According to "Interdum," Hancock correspondent for the *Peterborough Transcript*, generous donations from both local citizens and "many whose birth and early home was with us" paid for the project and helped ensure that the decorating scheme was consistent with that of the most fashionable interiors of the day.

A company from Newton Upper Falls, Massachusetts, did the decorative "painting, frescoing, and staining." As described by "Interdum":

> *The walls were painted terra cotta, with borders of olive green, defined by gilt lines; the dado a shade of red, decorated with a deeper red between dado and panels; the frieze a deeper shade of terra cotta than the sides, embellished with darker lines of red and gilt. The more elaborate decorations were reserved for the ceiling...divided into panels, with an elaborate centerpiece. The colors are shades of olive, warm yellow, terra cotta and ashes of roses. The pews are painted in olive green, with upholstery to match the dado in color. Carpets, shades of olive and red, to harmonize with the decorations. Windows—cathedral borders of red and amber, with figured ground glass centers.*

Heavy, dark mahogany furnishings were acquired and upholstered in olive plush. "The church interior, completely renovated and beautified, was universally admired, and the committee...received many well merited compliments for the fine taste displayed in the work."

There are no known images of the 1888 interior, and the stained-glass windows are hidden by exterior shutters in all existing photographs of the

Old Home Day in 1912.

meetinghouse. The painted ceiling was covered by the current metal one in 1904; the windows blew out in the Hurricane of 1938 and were replaced with clear glass. Although mostly obliterated by subsequent renovations, the 1888 Victorian paint scheme still remains on the woodwork behind the organ pipes in the northwest corner of the sanctuary, accessed through a removable door behind the choir loft.

## A Colonial Revival Village

Hancock's Main Street fits the typical image of a New England village, seemingly unchanged through time. White clapboard houses, a general store, a library and an inn line the street. A steepled meetinghouse faces a parklike Common. In reality, the appearance of Hancock's Main Street has changed dramatically since the village center was first established in the early nineteenth century. What we see today is mostly an idealized interpretation of what was perceived as "colonial" in the late nineteenth and early twentieth century Colonial Revival period.

The Colonial Revival movement was a product of American disillusionment with nineteenth-century industrialization, urbanization and immigration. Nostalgia grew for a more stable and less complicated past. The centennial celebration of 1876 inspired a nationalistic fervor, a reaffirmation of pride in America's national origins. Architectural preservation, renovation and new construction based on a romantic, sentimentalized and idealized image of "colonial" style became common. Builders and craftsmen incorporated the cultural values represented by the colonial style of architecture in both public buildings and private residences. One of the more common methods of achieving a colonial "look" was to revive the Greek Revival–inspired fashion of painting buildings white and adorning them with dark green or black exterior shutters, imitating the appearance of classical temples. Only the most elite features of colonial architecture were copied and incorporated into

The 1925 Colonial Revival addition to Hancock Town Library.

new and remodeled structures. The details were often further emphasized with greater size and prominence than the originals to make them appear "more colonial," hence more expressive of patriotic and nationalistic ideals. The resulting "colonial" villages were popularized and perpetuated in photo essay books and calendars, such as those by Samuel Chamberlain, who featured Hancock in his 1948 *Six New England Villages*.

Colonial Revival–inspired alterations are readily apparent in Hancock's village architecture. Examples are the front porch at 6 Main Street (the Peirce residence), the elaborate entry on 33 Main Street (home of Caitlin Mullins) and the portico on the John Hancock Inn. Most dramatic, however, is the colonial detailing of the 1925 addition to the Hancock Town Library. The earlier Victorian structure is almost completely obscured, serving merely as a link to the modern addition at the rear. Additional evidence of the enduring Colonial Revival influence is the widespread use of white paint and dark shutters, even on Victorian-era buildings, such as the home of the Klugs at 8 Main Street.

The Colonial Revival image of the New England village was less an accurate restoration of the early American landscape than an expression of longing for a mythical "golden age" in our country's past. Based more on the early nineteenth-century Greek Revival period than on actual colonial precedent, the New England architecture of this period may have originated as a negative reaction to modernization but it endures as an affirmation of shared cultural values. The Colonial Revival style has been extraordinarily successful in its persistence as the embodiment of the American cultural ideal. Those of us who take pride in Hancock's heritage can agree with Samuel Chamberlain: our town proves "there is such a thing as an American village, and that it is beautiful."

## The Clothespin Factory

Four streams running through Hancock once supported water-powered mills: Hosley, Ferguson, Davis and Moose Brooks. Beginning in 1780, when the first sawmill was built in town, these waterways powered "manufactories" that utilized the area's most abundant resource to produce a variety of woodenware, including pails, shingles, barrels, coffins, shutters, cabinets,

Sheldon Mill in 1940s. *Courtesy of Betsy Sheldon Salazar.*

bobbins and chairs. One mill, located on Hosley Brook at Old Dublin Road, was so successful that it once produced 218 hardwood clothespins per minute, enough to fill a railroad freight car every two and a half weeks, earning it the nickname: "The Clothespin Factory."

According to William W. Hayward's *History of Hancock, New Hampshire, 1764–1889*, John Newell built the first mill at that location in 1857. Considered a "remarkable mechanical genius," Newell operated a gristmill and sawmill and produced wooden pails and shingles, using a bucket-type water wheel twenty-four feet in diameter and eight feet in width to power machinery driven by wooden gears. According to Hayward, Newell was also notable in that he had "run a circular saw for fifty-two years without receiving an injury sufficient to draw blood" and because he was the first inventor of the spiral wire spring bed.

After a brief interval of ownership by George Davis, a manufacturer of apple barrels, the mill was purchased by Harry M. Sheldon in 1905. Sheldon was born in Hancock in 1879, the son of the enterprising Civil War veteran Charles Sheldon, who owned the prosperous farm across the street from the mill at 45 Old Dublin Road. According to Harry's son, Sime Sheldon, his father initially manufactured shingles, dowels, handles and other turned products, as well as ran a sawmill at the site. A large gasoline engine was soon installed to supplement the water power, and in 1910, the water wheel was replaced with a more efficient metal turbine. Sheldon also rebuilt the dam at Hunt's Pond, which served as the reservoir for the mill. By increasing the water storage capacity, Sheldon was able to generate more power for his thriving enterprise.

In 1915, the mill itself was enlarged and a steam boiler and engine installed; Sheldon began to produce wooden tent stakes for the army and hardwood clothespins, a household necessity. According to *The Second Hundred Years of Hancock, New Hampshire*, the town of Hancock voted in 1916 not to tax Sheldon for any improvements made on his mill for a five-year period, in appreciation of the steady employment the business provided for several local citizens and for its contribution to the war effort. The Boston & Maine Railroad installed a sidetrack adjacent to the mill to facilitate the shipping of its products; at its height, the operation generated an astonishing 33,984,000 clothespins per year. Hundreds of cords of beech, birch and rock maple logs were purchased locally and stored in the mill yards in the winter for future use, with two teamsters and two helpers employed outside, and eight men and seven girls working inside the mill.

In 1927, the Hancock Wood Products Company was incorporated and went public. According to the prospectus, the company offered its stock "as an attractive investment in what we believe to be one of the most prosperous wood products companies in the country." Proceeds from the sale were to be "devoted to the installation of new machinery for increasing production to meet an existing demand." By then, the majority of the clothespins were being sold wholesale to the J.J. Newberry Company, whose retail stores were located throughout New England and beyond, under the trade name of "New England Clothes Pins."

Sheldon married Alice Mae Fogg in 1903; they initially lived in the house directly opposite the mill, moving up the hill to the family's one-thousand-acre farm in 1918. Members of the Sheldon family have contributed a great deal to the community of Hancock over the years; Harry died in 1952, but his granddaughter, Betsy Sheldon Salazar, still lives in town. The business was sold to the Diamond Match Company in 1933, and all of the clothespin machinery was removed. Once advertised as "one of the largest of American manufacturers of clothes pins," with a "reputation for superiority in their field," Hancock's Clothespin Factory eventually fell into disrepair and was finally torn down.

# Hancock High "Aggies" Had Orchard on School Street

In 1917, Hancock High School celebrated its first graduating class and the completion of its commodious new building, located at the site of the present elementary school on School Street. The Hancock Educational Association, a group of citizens who believed that local children should have the opportunity to continue their educations beyond the eighth grade, ran Hancock High School from 1913 until its closure in 1954. In keeping with a nationwide trend, the high school placed an emphasis on agricultural instruction in its curriculum. Many Hancock residents at that time were also farmers or combined part-time farming with another occupation. The most productive local crop was apples, and the new high school had its own sixty-tree orchard.

Hancock's rugged terrain wasn't ideal for most forms of agriculture, but it was well suited to apple production. According to a 1959 talk given by longtime resident and local farmer Joe Quinn, for many years "apples were a good combination with any farm" and complemented the local production of milk and eggs. Hancock apples were shipped all over the world, with as many as 100,000 bushels shipped to Boston and New York and points beyond in a good year. Popular local varieties included Baldwin, Roxbury Russet, Winter Banana, Golden Russet, Macintosh and Tolman Sweet.

By 1925, the agricultural program was well established at Hancock High School. That year, the Hancock High School Agricultural Club published its first *Aggie Bulletin*, a slim booklet of articles on farming topics written by club members. Everett Adams and Walter Harrington submitted reports on their experiences growing potatoes, George Vatcher wrote about producing strawberries and Charles Gleason described the best method of feeding hens for winter production. There were articles on growing corn and alfalfa and on feeding workhorses and dairy cows in the winter. Chemistry was a popular course at the school, and the students enjoyed using their newfound knowledge to experiment with the application of chemical fertilizers and agricultural sprays to combat disease and insect pests. One popular spray combination, according to the *Aggie Bulletin*, included copper sulfate, lead arsenate and nicotine sulfate and was to be repeated at fourteen-day intervals. With the assistance of the local automobile garage, owned by

Hancock High School apple barrels.

W.M. Hanson, the students even designed and built their own horse-drawn sprayer for orchard use.

In addition to maintaining their own orchard and other crops, Hancock High School students actively marketed their produce and participated in the wider agricultural community. They attended statewide agricultural exhibitions to learn about the best methods of farming and profitable fruit production. Photographs in the archives of the Hancock Historical Society depict young men proudly showing off stacks of apple barrels ready for shipment, stenciled with the variety of apple contained within and the producer, Hancock High School.

By the mid-1930s, though, large-scale commercial apple production in Hancock ceased to be profitable as the cost of spraying for insect pests rose, the price of apples fell due to overproduction and freight train service to and from town was discontinued. Although many orchards were abandoned, remnants of them remain visible; trees from the old high school orchard still ornament the backyards of houses along School Street. Hancock High School continued to prepare its students for farming and other professional careers until 1954, when enrollment had slipped so low that the town voted to ship high school students to Peterborough rather than support its own high school.

Hancock High School's early agricultural emphasis reflected a nationwide effort to pique more individual interest in the profession of farming at an earlier age. One of the major spokesmen for this effort was an educator and prolific writer named H.P. Barrows, whose "Creed for Teaching of Agriculture" is quoted in *The Second Hundred Years of Hancock, New Hampshire*: "I believe that in agriculture we have a means of developing young people into better adults…I believe that productive agriculture is an excellent means of combining earning with living and learning."

# Part VII

# Everyday Life

## Postcards from Hancock

The first postcards printed with local views appeared in Hancock about 1900 as enterprising storeowners like W.D. Fogg and Edgar Ware took advantage of the flood of "summer visitors" arriving at local boardinghouses and farms. Brought to rural New England towns like Hancock by the arrival of reliable rail travel in the late 1800s, these visitors were delighted to buy postcards depicting local landmarks like the Common, the fountain, views of Main Street and the meetinghouse. In some of the earliest images, Main Street is a dirt road, rutted with buggy tracks, and the old, hand-lighted streetlamps are still visible.

The natural beauty of the area inspired postcards with images of Norway Pond and Nubanusit Lake, Moose Brook and Skatutakee and Monadnock Mountains. Vistas no longer clearly visible are displayed in views of Norway Pond from the depot and Main Street from the top of an open, rock-studded Norway Hill. Some of the landscape features recorded on postcards have since disappeared, such as the building that once housed the town's horse-drawn hearse, located at the foot of Pine Ridge Cemetery. Others have appeared, like the bandstand in views of the Common. Some landmarks have simply changed—the original covered bridge over the Contoocook

A postcard image of Main Street, printed by Edgar L. Ware.

River between Hancock and Greenfield washed away and was replaced in 1926; both bridges have been popular on postcards through the years.

Hancock's hotels and boardinghouses used postcards as advertising, from the fancy "Hancock Hotel" (now John Hancock Inn), where you could get a "smorgasbord supper" for one dollar in 1944, to the Forest House ("Just the place to spend your vacation and enjoy the clear fresh air that makes you eat, sleep and grow fat"). Mr. and Mrs. Gus Blanchett on Norway Hill used a postcard depicting their home (now the residence of Jeff Wilder and family) to advertise for "tourists."

Many summer visitors wrote messages about their travels; one card bears the relieved report that "we made the Elmwood change all right" prior to arriving and disembarking at the Hancock Depot. Postcards of local train stations were also popular; one depicts a very busy depot with a massive locomotive, stacks of poultry crates ready to be loaded and a patient old horse standing by with a two-seated buggy, probably ready to transport arriving visitors to their local destinations. Someone's "Aunt Mary" reported excitedly that they "had a chance to come over by Auto which was better than by [train] cars as we expected to." Other modes of travel persisted; the three-horse "Marlow" or "Hancock-Alstead" stagecoach was another popular postcard image.

Summer activities have long been featured on postcards; young women summering at Sargent Camp about 1917 are shown swimming, canoeing and riding horses. More recent postcards from the 1970s depict a busy beach at Norway Pond, with watchful mothers, attentive lifeguards and children of all ages enjoying the water. Regardless of the view, Hancock's postcards reflect surprisingly little real change over time. One young woman was pleased to conclude her 1910 vacation with the report that "[I] find everything about the same here. Will be leaving Monday afternoon on the 4 o'clock train."

## "Spring Never So Late"

The record snowfall of a few years ago resulted in a discouragingly late spring, with snow lingering much longer than usual on lawns and gardens. Yet there was at least one instance in the not-so-distant past when springtime must have seemed even more elusive. The following excerpt is from the May 3, 1956 issue of the *Peterborough Transcript*:

Schoolchildren make their way through deep snow to a mid-March town meeting in 1960.

*Norway Pond in Hancock village is frozen over the latest in at least 40 years, according to William M. Hanson, veteran fisherman and guide. He states that while he has known the ice to go out of the pond in March once, average time is from April 19 to the 21st. On Tuesday* [May 1], *the first day of the trout season, Mr. Hanson toured this entire area, but did not do any fishing nor see any fish caught. He corroborated the statement by Conservation Officer Kenneth Warren of Peterborough that all ponds in this vicinity are frozen over. The average thickness of ice is 15 inches. Charles Thomas of Dublin, town clerk and representative there, states that never has he seen so much snow in the woods nor ice on Dublin Lake so late in the year.*

## OUR WILD NEIGHBORS RETURN

When Hancock was first settled in the middle of the eighteenth century, there were many different species of wild animals here. Within one hundred years, however, several of these species had already completely disappeared from town, victims of the habitat devastation that accompanied large-scale land clearing or those that were hunted to the point of scarcity.

In the first volume of the 1888 *History of Hancock*, Reverend William Willis Hayward writes that wolves, catamounts (native wildcats or mountain lions), wildcats (probably bobcats), bear, deer and beaver, while numerous in the town's early days, had long since disappeared. For example, he notes that the last white-tailed deer shot in Hancock had been taken seventy years earlier, near the Antrim town line. As was common throughout much of New England at that time, large predators had been deliberately exterminated as early settlers sought to protect valuable livestock from wolves and bears. Hancock residents also played their part in the national decimation and eventual extinction of the passenger pigeon. Reverend Hayward notes that pigeon nets or stands were frequently set in town to capture and kill great numbers of these "numerous" birds, which could then be eaten or put away to be consumed later.

There is irony in the fact that, along with the steady rise in Hancock's human population since Reverend Hayward documented life here in the 1880s, there has been a concurrent increase in the numbers of wild animals

A moose cow with twin calves, taken at 22 Birch Road in 1995. *Courtesy of Nancy Adams.*

in town. White-tailed deer are no longer rare; in fact, their population is rapidly approaching the nuisance level, particularly for local gardeners and orchardists. And although some large predators have returned, most notably the black bear, the local wolf population seems to have been replaced by the coyote, which has assumed the role of most vexatious predator of livestock and family pets. Rumors of "catamount" sightings in Hancock surface now and again, and the beaver has returned to local waterways.

The regression of pastures to woodland, stricter hunting regulations and a general appreciation for and stewardship of local wildlife habitats have all contributed to the successful reestablishment of these species, our wild neighbors, Hancock's earliest "native" inhabitants.

## Hancock on Ice

Ask anyone who lived in Hancock during the 1970s what they liked most about winter back then, and you'll invariably trigger a flood of happy memories, many of them having to do with ice. Not the ice that periodically falls from the wintertime sky, robbing us of our power and destroying our trees, but the ice you skate on. For more than a decade, Hancock residents were lucky enough to enjoy outdoor ice skating on carefully maintained, lighted rinks every winter, thanks to the recreation committee and the hard work and generosity of two local retirees, Bob Stewart and Mert Knowles.

In 1969, the first public ice skating rink was built at the end of School Street, now the site of the Hancock Elementary School. That year's recreation committee—composed of Mrs. Richard Buck, Mrs. Joan Watson, Mrs. Anthony Brown, Otis Wilder Sr., Ernest Adams and Robert

Merton D. Knowles in 1981.

Stewart—raised funds to maintain and improve outdoor recreational facilities in town by raffling off a portable color television on Old Home Day. Work began on the first rink in October; within a year, a second rink had been added across the street, next to the ball field, so that recreational skaters wouldn't have to share the ice with hockey players.

For almost ten years, Bob and Mert, who lived nearby, got up early on cold, winter mornings and used hand-held hoses to flood the two rinks in the frigid hours before dawn. So no matter how vigorous the hockey game or how many figure skates had ground and chipped the ice, on most days we could expect a brand-new, glass-smooth surface for local skaters of all ages to enjoy. A year after the first rink was installed, Nancy Adams, Hancock correspondent for the *Peterborough Transcript*, reported that it was "the most popular place in town," with a steady crowd of skaters every weekend day and into the evenings, thanks to special light poles erected to illuminate the rinks each winter.

Hockey was particularly popular with the "young and not-so-old," Nancy reported in January 1970; there was at least one spirited pickup game for all ages most Saturday afternoons. She remembers carefully remaking snow pants for her young sons to accommodate their hockey pads; her husband, Bud, recalls a particularly intense adult game when he collided with another skater and was knocked out cold. My sisters and I remember many happy winter days spent skating with our friends, as well as the figure skating lessons taught by another generous and talented Hancock volunteer, Joyce Stevens.

There were "spoilers," of course—random acts of vandalism and the occasional mild winter—that sometimes made it difficult to maintain the rinks in good condition, but for the most part Hancock residents could count on skating at least part of every week from late December through February, maybe into March. And we could always look forward to chatting with Mert, or his ever-cheerful and friendly wife, Val, who would walk over from their house (now the home of David Drasba and Tammy Garre) to visit and remind us to check their garage for missing hats, mittens and skate guards.

By the late 1970s, however, Bob and Mert were finding it increasingly difficult to maintain the rinks. When they both "retired" from the task in 1978, the responsibility was initially assumed by "enthusiastic and energetic" local youths Mark Hamilton, Rick Adams, Mark and Jeff Wilder and Charlie and Shawn Kerwin, who hoped to keep the popular tradition going. But eventually the town deemed it necessary to discontinue the skating rinks, for ten years a place where local residents could get fresh air and exercise, engage in friendly, spirited competition and spend leisure time with neighbors and friends during the long months of winter.

## A NEW "GOLDEN AGE"?

In 1840, the town of Hancock, New Hampshire, was experiencing what would come to be remembered as the "Golden Age" of northern New England. With a population of 1,345 people, Hancock was a thriving community of farms, mills and retail establishments. There were nine school districts, each with its own one-room elementary school, and two secondary "academies" affiliated with the local Congregational and Baptist religious organizations. In the fifty years since the official founding of the town in 1790, the population had soared by 112 percent as land was cleared and settled. There was every indication that the town would continue to grow and prosper.

Only forty years later, however, the antebellum optimism had turned to despair. The tide of growth in New England had shifted from small, hillside farming communities to industrialized cities. By 1850, the population of Hancock had already decreased by 25 percent, to 1,012. The secession of part of the community to help create the town of Bennington in 1842 only accounted for part of the loss. As the West grew increasingly accessible after the Civil War, the steady trickle of population outflow became a torrent. When the town celebrated its centennial in 1879, the population of Hancock had already dwindled to 689, a decrease of 49 percent in less than forty years from its 1840 high. Those remaining in town were justifiably concerned about the situation. In his centennial address, published in *The History of Hancock, New Hampshire, 1764–1889*, Reverend William Willis Hayward blamed the frightening trend on "the unrest of our people, trying to subdue a continent in a generation," which had "sent many of [Hancock's] sons and daughters from her borders." As people moved away, houses and farms became vacant. "There is sadness in my heart," remarked Reverend Hayward, "when I remember that there are many deserted hearthstones within [Hancock's] limits."

An 1840 sketch of Hancock Common.

Hancock's population continued to shrink, decreasing a further 20 percent to reach its all-time low of 531 people in 1920. In the decade of the 1930s, however, the tide slowly began to turn. Outsiders bought the vacant farms and began using them as summer homes. The number of new, full-time residents began to increase following the Depression. By 1960, there were 722 people living in Hancock, many of them drawn here by new opportunities for employment in nearby Peterborough, working for companies such as New Hampshire Ball Bearings.

Hancock's natural beauty and remarkable architecture, complemented by its desirable, community-oriented way of life, stimulated population growth of over 25 percent per decade in the 1960s and 1970s. This prompted new concerns about different issues, such as the impact of rapid growth on the town's beauty and the preservation of its community spirit.

Hancock's population growth in the next century is hard to predict. The rate of increase slowed again between 1990 and 2000 to 12 percent, compared to the 30 percent growth rate of the previous decade. Whatever the numbers ultimately turn out to be, Reverend Hayward would surely be pleased and proud to know that Hancock had survived its nineteenth-century downturn to become the healthy, thriving community he had longed for so many years ago.

# Bibliography

Unpublished materials and newspaper clippings mentioned in the text but not cited below are from the archival collection of the Hancock Historical Society.

Barry, John M. *The Great Influenza: The Epic Story of the Deadliest Plague in History.* New York: Viking, 2004.

Chamberlain, Samuel. *Six New England Villages: Hancock, New Hampshire; Litchfield, Connecticut; Little Compton, Rhode Island; Old Bennington, Vermont; Old Deerfield, Massachusetts; Wiscasset, Maine.* New York: Hastings House, 1948.

Garvin, Donna-Belle. "James Hosley Whitcomb: New Hampshire Silhouettist." *Historical New Hampshire* 32, no. 1 and 2 (1977): 43–57.

Garvin, Donna-Belle, and James Garvin. *On the Road North of Boston: New Hampshire Taverns and Turnpikes, 1700–1900.* Hanover, NH: University Press of New England, 1988.

Goodwin, Doris Kearns. *No Ordinary Time: Franklin and Eleanor Roosevelt—The Home Front in World War II.* New York: Simon and Schuster, 1994.

Grew, Joseph C. *Turbulent Era: A Diplomatic Record of Forty Years, 1904–1945.* Edited by Walter Johnson, with assistance from Nancy Harvison Hooker. Boston: Houghton Mifflin, 1952.

Grieve, Mrs. M.A. *A Modern Herbal: The Medicinal, Culinary, Cosmetic and Economic Properties, Cultivation and Folklore of Herbs, Grasses, Fungi, Shrubs and Trees with all their Modern Scientific Uses.* Edited by Mrs. C.F. Leyel. 2 vols. Harcourt, Brace & Company, 1931. Reprint, New York: Dover, 1971.

Hancock History Committee, ed. *The Second Hundred Years of Hancock, New Hampshire.* Canaan, NH: Phoenix Publishing, 1979.

Hayward, William Willis. *The History of Hancock, New Hampshire, 1764–1889.* 2 vols. Lowell, MA: Vox Populi Press/S.W. Huse, 1889.

Martindale, Meredith. *Lilla Cabot Perry: An American Impressionist.* With Pamela Moffat. Washington, D.C.: National Museum of Women in the Arts, 1990.

Mitchell, Reid. *The Vacant Chair: The Northern Soldier Leaves Home.* New York: Oxford University Press, 1993.

Osgood, William E., and Leslie Hurley. *The Snowshoe Book.* Brattleboro, VT: Stephen Greene Press, 1971.

Pearson, Haydn S. *That Darned Minister's Son.* Garden City, NY: Doubleday, 1952.

*Peterborough Transcript.* Published by Transcript Printing Company. Accessed on microfilm at Peterborough Town Library, Peterborough, New Hampshire.

*Ratio Disciplinæ, or the Constitution of the Congregational Churches.* Portland, ME: Shirley and Hyde, 1829.

*Records of the Church of Christ of Hancock, Volume 1, Anno Domini 1792.* Town Archives, Hancock, New Hampshire.

Toumanoff, Vladimir I. Interview by William D. Morgan. Foreign Affairs Oral History Project: Foreign Affairs Series. Washington, D.C.: Association for Diplomatic Studies and Training, 2000.

Town of Hancock. *Annual Reports: Town of Hancock, New Hampshire.* Available at Hancock Town Library, Hancock Town Office Building and in the archives of the Hancock Historical Society.

# About the Author

Cynthia Amidon has a BA in history from Keene State College; she has also done graduate work at Fitchburg State College and Kent State University. She is an active community volunteer and freelance writer and lives with her husband, Gary Ryer, in her hometown of Hancock, New Hampshire. They are the parents of three grown children.

Visit us at
www.historypress.net